Tailored Gamification to Educational Technologies

Wilk Oliveira · Ig Ibert Bittencourt

Tailored Gamification to Educational Technologies

Springer

Wilk Oliveira
Institute of Mathematical
and Computer Sciences
University of São Paulo
São Carlos, São Paulo, Brazil

Ig Ibert Bittencourt
Computing Institute
Federal University of Alagoas
Maceió, Alagoas, Brazil

ISBN 978-981-32-9811-8 ISBN 978-981-32-9812-5 (eBook)
https://doi.org/10.1007/978-981-32-9812-5

This Springer imprint is published by the registered company Springer Nature Singapore Pte Ltd.
The registered company address is: 152 Beach Road, #21-01/04 Gateway East, Singapore 189721, Singapore

This book is dedicated to our families that supports us in all life projects.

Foreword

It is my great pleasure to introduce this book about *Tailored Gamification to Educational Technologies*, which is the result of in-depth research of different related issues for the use of gamification in education.

Gamification has become extremely popular as a research and application area, with various exciting application domains such as education and training, business, e-commerce, and entertainment. There has been an increasing interest in the research community on applying gamification to education systems. In this context, this book contributes to a growing interest in the field, as it expands the research advances on tailored gamification. Also, the book provides evidence regarding the selection of suitable gamification elements to different situations.

The book briefly introduces theoretical foundations in educational, psychological, and computational theories and discusses them regarding how gamification is related to each one. It serves as an overview of concepts and relevant topics to help understanding the importance of the gamification design and application. The heart of the book is the discussion of how gamification elements can be tailored for each situation. The authors propose a guideline to tailor a gamified educational system with the most suitable gamification elements based on the students' gamer type and gender. At the end of the book, the challenges and progress toward a deeper understanding of the field are detailed.

By situating gamification in the educational field, this book brings attention to the need to explore the benefits and possible drawbacks of gamification elements to each student's type and gender. The empirical study with MeuTutor shows how challenging it is to evaluate the gamification in an educational system, with Rigor, Reproducibility, and Responsibility.

I hope that you will enjoy reading this book as much as I did.

Santa Catarina, Brazil
May 2019

Isabela Gasparini

Preface

After seeing several studies, most of them theories about gamification, especially gamification in education, in the last 5 years, we are dedicated to conduct experimental researches on gamification applied to education. In particular, we are interested in observing the effects of gamification on students' behavior and learning, and how the effects can influence people's lives.

After several studies were conducted, as well as different scientific publications were made over the last few years, we thought it was time to work on a book that showed some of our experiences with gamification applied to education and that could contribute to the creation of new gamification design approaches.

Due to the number of publications, especially books on gamification in education currently available, we have tried to think of an unprecedented theme and with great openness to new studies. Given this background, we chose to deal with one of the topics of greater discussion at the time in this book: the personalization of gamification, a fundamental principle for the design of systems with greater power of persuasion.

In this book, we decided not to bother to conceptualize things that we consider to be basic to those who have already done some kind of research in gamification, and we tried to focus on what really matters for this book, that is, personalizing gamification. In this way, we will focus on discussing specific problems that gamification currently presents and how personalization can be a feasible alternative to face these problems.

In Chap. 1 of the book, we will briefly introduce the current problems related to gamification, passing quickly on the main objectives of gamification, its advantages, and its research challenges, to focus on the challenge of personalizing the gamification design and how this personalization can contribute to the design of educational systems and increase the students' learning.

In Chap. 2, we will discuss the main theories and approaches that contributed to the conception of the gamification and to the need for personalized gamification. We will focus on the theories/approaches coming from education (Behaviorism, Cognitivism, and Constructivism), psychology (positive psychology and persuasion strategies), and computer science (artificial intelligence and human–computer interaction). After this discussion, finally, we will be able to conceptualize the idea of tailored gamification.

Given this, in Chap. 3, we can then understand and discuss the state of the art in tailored gamification, through the presentation and discussion of several studies that directly or indirectly contributed to this domain. From the presentation and discussion of these studies, we will, in fact, be able to understand the challenges that lie behind personalization of gamification.

In Chap. 4, we will begin to leave the theoretical field for a practical approach. We will present, in this chapter, a proposal for a computational approach to personalize gamified educational systems, which was built through several studies carried out in recent years.

In Chap. 5, deepening our practical approach, we will present a study where, through an experiment, we identified the most suitable gamification elements according to the students' gamer type and gender. We will also present the evaluation of the study conducted by us and a discussion of the results based on the topics presented in previous chapters.

In Chap. 6, further deepening our practical approach, we present a practical application, that is, a personalized educational system based on the approach previously proposed in the book, showing from the design principles of the original system (not personalized) to the tailored screens based on users' gamer types.

Finally, in Chap. 7 and Appendix, we will discuss the topics presented in the book, as well as present and discuss the challenges that still need to be faced in this field, as well as the opportunities and research directions generated by these challenges.

São Carlos, SP, Brazil — Wilk Oliveira
Maceió, AL, Brazil — Ig Ibert Bittencourt
May 2019

Acknowledgements

We would like to thank and dedicate this book to our families, for the unconditional support and affection during all the moments, and to our friends and colleagues for the meetings and discussions that culminated in the writing of this book.

Contents

About the Authors

Prof. Wilk Oliveira holds a master's degree in Computer Science from the Federal University of Alagoas (Brazil), with an exchange program at the University of Saskatchewan (Canada). He completed a bachelor's degree in Computer Science and Pedagogy at the University of Pernambuco (Brazil). He is a Ph.D. student at the University of São Paulo (Brazil) and researcher at the Laboratory of Applied Computer Science to Advanced Social Technology and Education (University of São Paulo). Wilk Oliveira was a researcher at the Center of Excellence for Social Technologies (Federal University of Alagoas) and the Multi-Agent Distributed Mobile and Ubiquitous Computing Lab (University of Saskatchewan). He was also an assistant professor in the Postgraduate Program in Management of the Tiradentes University (Brazil), and in the Postgraduate Program in Computer Science and Computational Mathematics of the University of São Paulo (Brazil).

Prof. Ig Ibert Bittencourt is an Associate Professor at the Federal University of Alagoas (Brazil) and Co-Director of the Center of Excellence for Social Technologies. He received his Ph.D. in Computer Science from the Federal University of Campina Grande (Brazil) in 2009 and a postdoctoral degree in Computer Science from the University of Campinas (UNICAMP, Brazil) in 2013. During his Ph.D., he proposed a theoretical and computational model to build semantic web-based educational systems. Professor Ig Bittencourt's research career has been devoted to artificial intelligence in education (AIED), working on the design, development, and experimentation of educational technologies. He was the President of the Brazilian Computer Society's Special Committee on Computers and Education (leading around 2500 researchers). Professor Ig Bittencourt co-founded MeuTutor—an innovative company in the field of educational technology in Brazil.

Acronyms

ACM	Association for Computing Machinery
AI	Artificial intelligence
AIED	Artificial Intelligence in Education
ANOVA	One-way analysis of variance
C&E	Computers and education
CLS	Collaborative learning scenarios
CSS	Cascading Style Sheets
EEG	Electroencephalogram
HCI	Human–computer interaction
HTML	Hypertext Markup Language
ITS	Intelligent educational systems
PACM	Player Archetype Change Management
PHP	Hypertext Preprocessor
PT	Persuasive technology
SLR	Systematic literature review
TGES	Tailored gamified educational systems
UX	User experience
VLE	Virtual learning environments

Chapter 1
Introduction

Abstract In recent years, many conducted studies have been using game design elements in educational systems to improve student's experience and learning in the systems. Although many studies have shown excellent results with respect to student learning, several other studies have shown that gamification, when not properly planned, developed, and applied, can cause negative outcomes, such as demotivation and disengagement, which may even lead to students dropping out of the courses they are doing. One of the main suspects of this problem is the fact that most systems are not personalized according to student preferences and feature several gamification elements, some of which students may not like and feel unmotivated. Thus, the concept of tailored gamification appeared, that is, gamification planned according to the preferences and needs of the students. Throughout this chapter, we will present and discuss some problems related to gamification and introduce the importance of providing tailored systems according to students' preferences, aiming to bring the students to a better learning experience.

1.1 From Gamification Theory to Tailored Gamification

In the past few years, different digital technologies have emerged in various fields, such as social networks [1], movies [2], health [3], and educational fields [4–6], drawing the attention of academics and practitioners. In the educational field, several studies have used digital technologies with many different goals, such as improving students' concentration, engagement, and flow experience [7], also providing recommendation of educational resources to the students [8, 9] and offering an adaptive system [10, 11]. These studies have brought different challenges and opportunities to the industry and to the Computer and Education community (C&E), with a preference for educational environments design capable of providing personalized learning to the students, according to their personal characteristics and preferences [10, 12, 13].

Commonly, many different digital technologies have been used in the educational field (e.g., educational games [4], intelligent tutoring systems [14], adaptive hypermedia systems [15], and educational systems [16–18], to solve big notorious

W. Oliveira and I. I. Bittencourt, *Tailored Gamification to Educational Technologies*,
https://doi.org/10.1007/978-981-32-9812-5_1

challenges in this field (e.g., students' evasion, frustration, demotivation, among others), as well as provide innovative solutions that can solve problems on a large scale, reaching a large number of students in a positive way.

In order to provide educational resources to the students in different geographical contexts with distinct educational goals, a growing number of studies have been developing and evaluating different kinds of educational systems. For instance, they used recommended agents based on the students' learning styles [6], or measured the students' experience in this kind of system [19]. These studies have highlighted the importance of educational systems as a kind of system capable of helping students and teachers in different perspectives that include allowing students to learn any content in different time zones and geographical locations, as well as allowing them to work in a collaborative way and to receive only specific contents according to their individual needs [6, 20, 21].

Besides, the educational systems represent an important way to provide solutions to some major educational problems (i.e., students' evasion, disengagement, and demotivation). Recent empirical experimental studies showed contradictory results regarding the efficacy of these systems, such as students' evasion and demotivation during the virtual course [22, 23]. This situation surprised many researchers in the scientific community and drew the attention of researchers who have sought solutions to these problems.

In order to begin to solve the problem of students' evasion, disengagement, and demotivation in the educational systems, recent researches have used game and gamification elements associated with its activities, in order to decrease students' the problems before presented, as well as to improve student's concentration, engagement, and learning in the educational systems [23–25]. These studies have been implementing and evaluating the use of gamification design in the educational systems, raising the concept of gamified educational systems.

Recent results have shown that these systems are capable of offering different ways for the students to perform the educational activities associated with game design elements [26–28]. They also showed that gamified educational systems could provide a number of benefits to students (i.e., increasing students' motivation [29, 30] and increasing students' performance and learning [31, 32]).

However, similar studies are showing that, in many cases, the use of gamification in an educational context (especially gamified educational systems) does not always improve the students' motivation, engagement, and learning [26, 33, 34]. It also surprised many researchers and draws the attention of the community for the need of deeper researches, especially in order to identify when and how the use of gamification is really effective to improve the students' satisfaction with the system and to propose solutions in order to provide better gamification in the moments in which the gamification has not had good effects on students' learning outcomes.

More recent studies in the field of gamified educational systems, conducted since early 2013, also have shown contradictory results, pointing to the fact that sometimes gamified educational systems improve the students' learning outcomes, but sometimes the same system does not improve or even, in some cases, decrease the students' motivation, engagement, and learning, causing frustrations, demotivation, or disengagement of the students [2, 33]. Studies conducted in the last years (e.g., [33, 35, 36]) have highlighted that this situation may occur often because students that use the gamified educational systems have different behavior, expectations, and needs; thus, they are encouraged in different ways [10, 23].

In gamified educational systems, it is important to consider that the students have different genders, ages, and gamer types, so they are more motivated or less motivated in different ways, according to their preferences and the gamification elements (gamification design) used in the system [3, 10, 35]. For instance, considering the different students' gamer types, if a student is competitive, it is more likely that he prefers to earn points and compete in missions. Also, the same student might be demotivated to participate in collaborative or interactive activities, needing to participate in specific activities, associated with their preference or gamer type [10, 31, 33].

Thus, depending on the gamification design used in these systems, the final results can be harmful to the students' motivation, engagement, flow experience, and such [33, 37, 38]. According to these studies, if the system provides the same gamification elements to all participants (*one-size-fits-all* approach), without considering their individual characteristics (e.g., gamer type) it might generate both a positive effect on some students and a negative effect on others.

Highlighting this problem, according to some recent secondary studies [31, 39–41], most of the gamified educational systems created have provided different gamification elements to students, such as Points, Badges, Trophies, and Ranking. However, unfortunately, these systems are using the *one-size-fits-all* approach or monolithic group [33], which may become harmful to students. In other words, because of the use of the same gamification elements to all of the students, this has to cause the opposite effect from what is intended for this kind of system. This problem highlights the recent big challenge presented by [10, 33, 42] and others, of creating tailored systems, based on the students' needs and preferences.

Some recent studies have conducted researches to solve this problem [24, 33, 35, 43–46]. These studies are generally conducted to provide theoretical relationships between various personality types and traits, as well as outlined player typologies that currently exist, or to provide toolboxes to better inform the design of gamified systems and specifically target users in a more internally engaging and motivating way [24]. Other recent important advances are the identification of the best persuasive strategies associated with each gamer type, and the development of a guideline to tailor gamified systems based on the users' gamer types [33, 35, 43].

Besides these recent advances, this field has many open challenges and gaps to be solved [3, 10, 24, 47, 48]. Most of the studies conducted in the last years were made in different fields other than the educational (i.e., specific studies for marketing or health sciences). It created a gap in the field on education, as well as opened an opportunity to conduct similar studies in the area. Recent studies identified which are the best persuasive strategies associated with each gamer type. Another big challenge in this field is to provide a process and a structure so that the gamification designers will be able to implement gamified educational systems, tailor it, and take as basis the students' gamer types, using the best game design element to each student gamer type.

Based on the recent challenges to provide adapted gamified educational systems for each student [3, 10, 24, 47, 48], this book aims to introduce and explore the field of tailored gamified educational technologies. The book presents a theoretical view of this domain, including some related psychological and educational theories and a complete state-of-the-art analysis on this topic. The book also presents an approach to tailor this kind of system based on the students' gamer type and students' gender, showing results of empirical experiments on these approaches, as well as it presents a guideline to tailor gamified educational systems based on students' gamer types and gender. The book will also present a second guideline with the best, the neuter, and the worst gamification elements to motivate each student's gamer type and gender.

The book is structured as follows: The second chapter will present the theoretical foundation that involves the importance of tailored gamification, including psychological, pedagogical, and computational aspects. The third chapter presents a state of the art on tailored gamification, showing the latest studies conducted in this domain and discussing its results. The fourth chapter will begin the more practical part of the book and show practical approaches to tailoring the gamification in educational systems. The fifth chapter will present an empirical study that sought to relate the gamification elements most suitable to each gamer type and gender. The sixth chapter will present a gamified educational system that was tailored according to the approaches presented in the previous chapters, showing the whole step by step developed for the tailoring of the system, as well as presenting different lessons learned during the customization of the system. Finally, the seventh chapter shows the concluding remarks, making a general analysis of challenges and opportunities in the area of tailored gamification for educational systems to be addressed in the coming decade.

References

1. I. Adaji, K. Oyibo, J. Vassileva, The effect of gender and age on the factors that influence healthy shopping habits in e-commerce, in *Proceedings of the 26th Conference on User Modeling, Adaptation and Personalization* (ACM, 2018), pp. 251–255
2. W. Wu, L. Chen, Implicit acquisition of user personality for augmenting movie recommendations, in *International Conference on User Modeling, Adaptation, and Personalization* (Springer, 2015), pp. 302–314
3. R. Orji, R.L. Mandryk, J. Vassileva, K.M. Gerling, Tailoring persuasive health games to gamer type, in *Proceedings of the SIGCHI Conference on Human Factors in Computing Systems* (ACM, 2013), pp. 2467–2476
4. T.M. Connolly, E.A. Boyle, E. MacArthur, T. Hainey, J.M. Boyle, A systematic literature review of empirical evidence on computer games and serious games. Comput. Educ. **59**(2), 661–686 (2012)
5. I.I. Bittencourt, E. Costa, M. Silva, E. Soares, A computational model for developing semantic web-based educational systems. Knowl. Based Syst. **22**(4), 302–315 (2009)

6. M.-I. Dascalu, C.-N. Bodea, A. Moldoveanu, A. Mohora, M. Lytras, P.O. de Pablos, A recommender agent based on learning styles for better virtual collaborative learning experiences. Comput. Hum. Behav. **45**, 243–253 (2015)
7. J. Hamari, D.J. Shernoff, E. Rowe, B. Coller, J. Asbell-Clarke, T. Edwards, Challenging games help students learn: an empirical study on engagement, flow and immersion in game-based learning. Comput. Hum. Behav. **54**, 170–179 (2016)
8. O. Holanda, R. Ferreira, E. Costa, I.I. Bittencourt, J. Melo, M. Peixoto, W. Tiengo, Educational resources recommendation system based on agents and semantic web for helping students in a virtual learning environment. Int. J. Web Based Communities **8**(3), 333–353 (2012)
9. G.F. Tondello, R. Orji, L.E. Nacke, Recommender systems for personalized gamification, in *Adjunct Publication of the 25th Conference on User Modeling, Adaptation and Personalization* (ACM, 2017), pp. 425–430
10. J. Masthoff, J. Vassileva, Tutorial on personalization for behaviour change, in *Proceedings of the 20th International Conference on Intelligent User Interfaces* (ACM, 2015), pp. 439–442
11. C.S. González, P. Toledo, V. Muñoz et al., Enhancing the engagement of intelligent tutorial systems through personalization of gamification. Int. J. Eng. Educ. **32**(1), 532–541 (2016)
12. M. Busch, E.E. Mattheiss, W. Hochleitner, C. Hochleitner, M. Lankes, P. Fröhlich, R. Orji, M. Tscheligi, Using player type models for personalized game design-an empirical investigation. IxD&A **28**, 145–163 (2016)
13. A. Ciocarlan, J. Masthoff, N. Oren, Qualitative study into adapting persuasive games for mental wellbeing to personality, stressors and attitudes, in *Adjunct Publication of the 25th Conference on User Modeling, Adaptation and Personalization* (ACM, 2017), pp. 402–407
14. B.P. Woolf, *Building Intelligent Interactive Tutors: Student-centered Strategies for Revolutionizing E-learning* (Morgan Kaufmann, Burlington, 2010)
15. P. Brusilovsky, M.T. Maybury, From adaptive hypermedia to the adaptive web. Commun. ACM **45**(5), 30–33 (2002)
16. P. Dillenbourg, D. Schneider, P. Synteta, Virtual learning environments, in *3rd Hellenic Conference on "Information & Communication Technologies in Education"*, Kastaniotis Editions, Greece (2002), pp. 3–18
17. N. Kerimbayev, Virtual learning: possibilities and realization. Educ. Inf. Technol. **21**(6), 1521–1533 (2016)
18. S.J. de Santana, H.A. Souza, V.A. Florentin, R. Paiva, I.I. Bittencourt, S. Isotani, A quantitative analysis of the most relevant gamification elements in an online learning environment, in *Proceedings of the 25th International Conference Companion on World Wide Web*, pp. 911–916. International World Wide Web Conferences Steering Committee (2016)
19. D. Janßen, C. Tummel, A. Richert, I. Isenhardt, Towards measuring user experience, activation and task performance in immersive virtual learning environments for students, in *International Conference on Immersive Learning* (Springer, 2016), pp. 45–58
20. G.C. Challco, D.A. Moreira, I.I. Bittencourt, R. Mizoguchi, S. Isotani, Personalization of gamification in collaborative learning contexts using ontologies. IEEE Lat. Am. Trans. **13**(6), 1995–2002 (2015)
21. R. Paiva, I.I. Bittencourt, T. Tenório, P. Jaques, S. Isotani, What do students do on-line? Modeling students' interactions to improve their learning experience. Comput. Hum. Behav. **64**, 769–781 (2016)
22. M. Alencar, E. Santos, J.F. Netto, Identifying students with evasion risk using data mining, in *EdMedia: World Conference on Educational Media and Technology*, pp. 611–616. Association for the Advancement of Computing in Education (AACE) (2015)
23. R.O.A. Paiva, I.I. Bittencourt, A.P. da Silva, S. Isotani, P. Jaques, Improving pedagogical recommendations by classifying students according to their interactional behavior in a gamified learning environment, in *Proceedings of the 30th Annual ACM Symposium on Applied Computing* (ACM, 2015), pp. 233–238
24. L.S. Ferro, S.P. Walz, S. Greuter, Towards personalised, gamified systems: an investigation into game design, personality and player typologies, in *Proceedings of The 9th Australasian Conference on Interactive Entertainment: Matters of Life and Death* (ACM, 2013), p. 7

25. D. Dermeval, J. Vilela, I.I. Bittencourt, J. Castro, S. Isotani, P. Brito, A systematic review on the use of ontologies in requirements engineering, in *2014 Brazilian Symposium on Software Engineering (SBES)* (IEEE, 2014), pp. 1–10
26. J. Hamari, J. Koivisto, H. Sarsa, Does gamification work?–a literature review of empirical studies on gamification, in *2014 47th Hawaii International Conference on System Sciences (HICSS)* (IEEE, 2014), pp. 3025–3034
27. J. Hamari, J. Tuunanen, Player types: a meta-synthesis. Trans. Digit. Games Res. Assoc. **1**(2) (2014)
28. J. Hamari, Do badges increase user activity? A field experiment on the effects of gamification. Comput. Hum. Behav. (2015)
29. R. Cózar-Gutiérrez, J.M. Sáez-López, Game-based learning and gamification in initial teacher training in the social sciences: an experiment with minecraftedu. Int. J. Educ. Technol. High. Educ. **13**(1), 2 (2016)
30. J. Vassileva, Motivating participation in social computing applications: a user modeling perspective. User Model. User Adapt. Interact. **22**(1), 177–201 (2012)
31. F.F.-H. Nah, Q. Zeng, V.R. Telaprolu, A.P. Ayyappa, B. Eschenbrenner, Gamification of education: a review of literature, in *International Conference on HCI in Business* (Springer, 2014), pp. 401–409
32. L.Z. Pedro, A.M. Lopes, B.G. Prates, J. Vassileva, S. Isotani. Does gamification work for boys and girls?: an exploratory study with a virtual learning environment, in *Proceedings of the 30th Annual ACM Symposium on Applied Computing* (ACM, 2015), pp. 214–219
33. R. Orji, Design for behaviour change: a model-driven approach for tailoring persuasive technologies. Ph.D. Thesis (2014)
34. G.F. Tondello, L.E. Nacke, Towards customizing gameful systems by gameful design elements, in *PPT@ PERSUASIVE* (2018), pp. 102–110
35. B. Monterrat, É. Lavoué, S. George, Toward an adaptive gamification system for learning environments, in *International Conference on Computer Supported Education* (Springer, 2014), pp. 115–129
36. M. Alhathli, J. Masthoff, A. Siddharthan, Should learning material's selection be adapted to learning style and personality? in *Adjunct Publication of the 25th Conference on User Modeling, Adaptation and Personalization* (ACM, 2017), pp. 275–280
37. C. Bateman, R. Lowenhaupt, L. Nacke, Player typology in theory and practice, in *DiGRA Conference* (2011)
38. N. Yee, Motivations of play in MMORPGs: results from a factor analytic approach. The Daedalus Project (2005)
39. A. Matallaoui, J. Koivisto, J. Hamari, R. Zarnekow. How effective is "exergamification" a systematic review on the effectiveness of gamification features in exergames, in *Proceedings of the 50th Hawaii International Conference on System Sciences* (2017)
40. S. de Sousa Borges, V.H. Durelli, H.M. Reis, S. Isotani, A systematic mapping on gamification applied to education, in *Proceedings of the 29th Annual ACM Symposium on Applied Computing* (ACM, 2014), pp. 216–222
41. L. Dalmina, J.L.V. Barbosa, H.D. Vianna, A systematic mapping study of gamification models oriented to motivational characteristics. Behav. Inf. Technol. 1–18 (2019)
42. B. Monterrat, M. Desmarais, E. Lavoué, S. George, A player model for adaptive gamification in learning environments, in *International Conference on Artificial Intelligence in Education* (Springer, 2015), pp. 297–306
43. W.O. Santos, I.I. Bittencourt, J. Vassileva, Design of tailored gamified educational systems based on gamer types, in *Anais dos Workshops do Congresso Brasileiro de Informática na Educação*, vol. 7 (2018), p. 42
44. A. Mora, G.F. Tondello, L.E. Nacke, J. Arnedo-Moreno, Effect of personalized gameful design on student engagement, in *2018 IEEE Global Engineering Education Conference (EDUCON)* (IEEE, 2018), pp. 1925–1933
45. R. Orji, G.F. Tondello, L.E. Nacke, Personalizing persuasive strategies in gameful systems to gamification user types, in *Proceedings of the 2018 CHI Conference on Human Factors in Computing Systems* (ACM, 2018), p. 435

46. D. Rajanen, M. Rajanen, Personalized gamification: a model for play data profiling, in *DDGD@ MindTrek* (2017), pp. 26–33
47. M. Böckle, J. Novak, M. Bick, Towards adaptive gamification: a synthesis of current developments (2017)
48. F. de Vette, M. Tabak, H.J. Hermens, M. Vollenbroek, Mapping game preferences of older adults: a field study towards tailored gamified applications, in *Proceedings of the 10th Nordic Conference on Human-Computer Interaction* (ACM, 2018), pp. 93–101

Chapter 2
Theoretical Foundations

Abstract Since the onset of the term gamification, many studies have tried to understand the theories that involve gamification, relating it to different theoretical backgrounds. Concerning gamification applied to educational systems, the range of theories becomes even greater, since it involves theories related to education (e.g., Behaviorism, Cognitivism, and Constructivism), psychology (e.g., Flow Theory and persuasion), and computer science (e.g., artificial intelligence and human–computer interaction). With that said, in this chapter, we aim to present a range of theories that interconnect the tailored gamification. In this chapter, we do not intend to rediscuss topics that have already been addressed in recent articles on gamification, but to force on Points that are not normally addressed, as well as on topics directly linked to personalization of gamification. Finally, we will also try to conceptualize the idea of tailored gamification.

2.1 Educational Theories

Over the years, several scholars have sought to discuss different theoretical strategies in education. In general, the vast majority of these theories are independent of any technology, that is, regardless of which technologies are used in education, the discourses on these theories remain valid. This section aims to present different educational theories and their relation with gamification. Our aim is not to deepen the discussion of these theories, since there are several specific studies that deepen each one of them, our objective is to present an introduction to each theory and to discuss its relations with gamification (specially, tailored gamification). In this section, we will present a discussion on *(i)* Behaviorism, *(ii)* Cognitivism, and *(iii)* Constructivism.

2.1.1 Behaviorism

In general, the Behaviorism represents a systematic approach to understanding the behavior of humans and other animals, combining elements of philosophy, method-

W. Oliveira and I. I. Bittencourt, *Tailored Gamification to Educational Technologies*,
https://doi.org/10.1007/978-981-32-9812-5_2

ology, and psychological theory [1, 2]. The Behaviorism was founded by Skinner who discovered that behaviors could be shaped when the use of reinforcement was implemented [3].

In education, the idea of Behaviorism is on to change in external behavior achieved through the use of reinforcement and repetition (rote learning) to shape learners' behavior [4]. According to Nagowah and Nagowah [5], within the behaviorist view of learning, the "teacher" is the dominant person in the classroom and takes complete control, the evaluation of learning comes from the teacher who decides what is right or wrong.

So, the conceptualization of learning, using the Behaviorism, is not interested in the internal processes of learning to lead to behavior change and has no place for the emotions involved in the process [5–7]. Because of this focus on behavior change, without necessarily focusing on the processes involved in this change, many researchers have invested in the use of techniques that can change student's behavior in educational settings through the behavioral change theories.

At the same time, the idea of gamification can be seen as contradicting the central idea of Behaviorism as a conceptualization in education, since according to Nagowah and Nagowah [5], in Behaviorism the teacher has an absolute role. This, therefore, the emancipation of the student, leaves them free to choose the path that they can follow, independent of the instructor position.

On the other hand, gamification is totally linked to the idea of Behaviorism from the point of view of being used as a strategy to change students' behavior in relation to learning. Especially with the emergence of behavior change theories presented earlier, many researchers have conducted studies to look at the ability of gamification to alter students' behavior in educational settings.

Considering the aforementioned aspects, the main relation between gamification (especially personalized gamification) and Behaviorism consists in the practical use of gamification as a strategy to change students' behavior, for example, by helping a student who may have difficulty staying engaged in an educational environment, the engagement can be increased without necessarily worrying about the mental processes that lead to engagement.

2.1.2 Cognitivism

The idea of Cognitivism is to understand the mind that gained credence through a theoretical framework and was proposed as a response to the Behaviorism idea, which was reported as neglected to explain cognition. The cognitive psychology is derived from the word cognoscere (Latin), and referring to the knowing and information, being a psychological information-processing derived in from the traditions of the research of problem solving [8, 9].

Unlike Behaviorism, the Cognitivism keeps the focus on the mind processes, aiming to understand how the person perceive, think, remember, learn, solve problems, and direct their attention to one stimulus rather than another. Specially, related to learn, Cognitivism focuses on the inner mental activities, in other words, opening the "black box" of the human mind for understanding how people learn, exploring the thinking, memory, knowing, and problem solving [10, 11].

Jean Piaget [12] was the first psychologist to make a systematic study of cognitive development. His contributions include a stage theory of child cognitive development, detailed observational studies of cognition in children, and a series of simple but ingenious tests to reveal different cognitive abilities [13]. To Piaget, the cognitive employment is a progressive reorganization of the mental processes from a biological maturation and environmental experience.

According to distinct Piaget studies [12, 14, 15], the assimilation and accommodation require an active learner, and not a passive one. In this sense, the problem-solving skills cannot be taught, they must be discovered. In a educational setting, the learning should be student-centered and accomplished through active discovery learning. The role of the instructor is to facilitate learning, rather than direct tuition.

The central idea of gamification, especially of personalized gamification, is largely tied to the idea of Piaget's Cognitivism. It is a strategy that seeks to make the students independent, they become active beings in search of the learning process and understand that the individual characteristics should be considered in this process. In this way, tailored gamification can be considered a strategy to put into practice the ideas of Cognitivism.

2.1.3 Constructivism

The Constructivism could be explained as a learning theory found in psychology, which studies how people might acquire knowledge and learn, directly applied to education, suggesting that humans construct knowledge and meaning from their experiences [16–18]. The prominent theorist is Jean Piaget, who focused on how humans develop meaning in relation to the interaction between their experiences and their ideas. The idea of Constructivism does not refer to a specific pedagogy, although it is often confused with Constructionism (Seymour Papert).

The Constructivism suggests that learners build knowledge out of their experiences, associated with pedagogical approaches that promote active learning, or "learning by doing." It argues that the responsibility of learning should reside increasingly with the learner [16–18], emphasizing the importance of students being actively involved in the learning process.

Strongly influenced by Vygotsky's study, the Constructivism argues that knowledge is first constructed in a social context and is then appropriated by individuals [19]. The process of sharing individual perspectives (called collaborative elaboration) results in learners constructing understanding together that would not be possible alone [19–21].

The original idea of using gamification in education has a direct relationship with Constructivism. Especially, for propose that the gamification is used to provide a way for learners to construct knowledge out of their experiences, associating pedagogical approaches and transferring to the learner the responsibility of learning. In a special way, tailored gamification is more associated with the idea of Constructivism, seeking to consider the social context of learners and the individualities of students in the learning process.

2.2 Psychological Theories

Similar to educational theories, gamification, in particular, tailored gamification, appropriates theories from psychology, or makes use of these theories as a way of organizing and proposing its principles. Over the years, researchers have sought to discuss gamification and their relationships to psychology theories, as well as conducting experimental studies toward identifying the relationships between actions and behaviors of individuals regarding the use of gamification systems. In this section, we will discuss some theories of psychology and its relations with gamification. Our idea, again, is not to deepen the theories but to present the theory in general and discuss its relations with gamification. We will focus on the following theories: *(i)* Flow Theory and *(ii)* persuasive strategies.

2.2.1 Flow Theory

The idea of "flow experience" or "flow state" was created by a Hungarian psychologist named Mihalyi Csikszentmihalyi [22] as a technical term to define a good feeling or "optimal experience" that a person can have as a motivating action in their daily activities, such as at work, sports practice, or artistic activities Faiola et al. [23]. According to Faiola, the key to understanding the "flow" is the "autotelic experience" concept (from the ancient Greek $\alpha\upsilon\tau o\tau\varepsilon\lambda\eta\varsigma$, or "self-goal"). Thus, the autotelic experience is the result produced by an activity or situation that provides its own intrinsic motivation, rewards, or incentives, specifically without any outside goals or rewards.

Since the establishment of the basis of Csikszentmihalyi's Flow Theory, several approaches have been proposed aiming to describe this kind of experience. Csikszentmihalyi [22] describes nine required dimensions for an activity to prompt the flow experience: (1) the goals need to be clear; (2) the feedback needs to be immediate; (3) need a match between skills and challenges; (4) need a merger of action and awareness; (5) need to facilitate the concentration on the task at hand; (6) aid a sense of control; (7) a loss of self-consciousness during the task is need; (8) the sense of time changed; and (9) the experience need becoming "autotelic."

In order to an activity lead a person to flow state, it should provide a balance between challenge's level and ability required for the person to complete a task. If the difficulty of a challenge is greater than the person's skill level, he/she gets

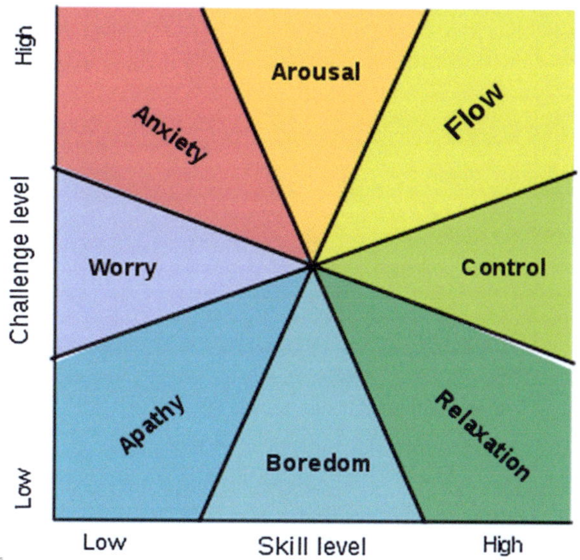

Fig. 2.1 Original Csikszentmihalyi [22] flow model (Wikipedia)

anxious. By contrast, if the difficulty of the challenge is less than the person's ability, it tends to be a boring activity Admiraal et al. [24].

Over the time, different conceptual models have been proposed aiming to describe the concept of flow state. These conceptual models also establish parameters to measure the flow state level, through flow state scales and other instruments. Csikszentmihalyi [22] was the first researcher to propose a model to describe flow state. He proposed the flow as an emotional state located between anxiety/arousal and relaxation/control (see Fig. 2.1). In the first model, Csikszentmihalyi describes flow as an emotional state that people can feel during specific activities, especially activities that provide a balance between people's skill level and activity's challenge level and immediate feedback.

Some years later, new researches have been conducted and new models have been proposed. Csikszentmihalyi proposed a new model (see Fig. 2.2a) based on the first one, which represents a simplification model, synthesizing the skill–challenge balance to flow state [25]. Afterward, other researchers proposed different flow models and representations (all based on the Csikszentmihalyi's flow models) [25]. Schell [26] proposed a slightly different model (see Fig. 2.2b) on which flow state can vary in each person, and the flow state level can be higher or lower at different times of the activity [25]. More recently, Sala [27] addressed flow state by dividing it into different modules (worlds), on which each state is located in a different slice of time (see Fig. 2.2c). Furthermore, Massimini and Carli [28] proposed a flow model that separates the flow components in different channels (see Fig. 2.2d).

The flow state can be considered the "golden pot at the end of the rainbow" by game designers, meaning that it is the wish of all game designers, teachers, and instructors that their students can achieve the flow state in the gamified educational systems.

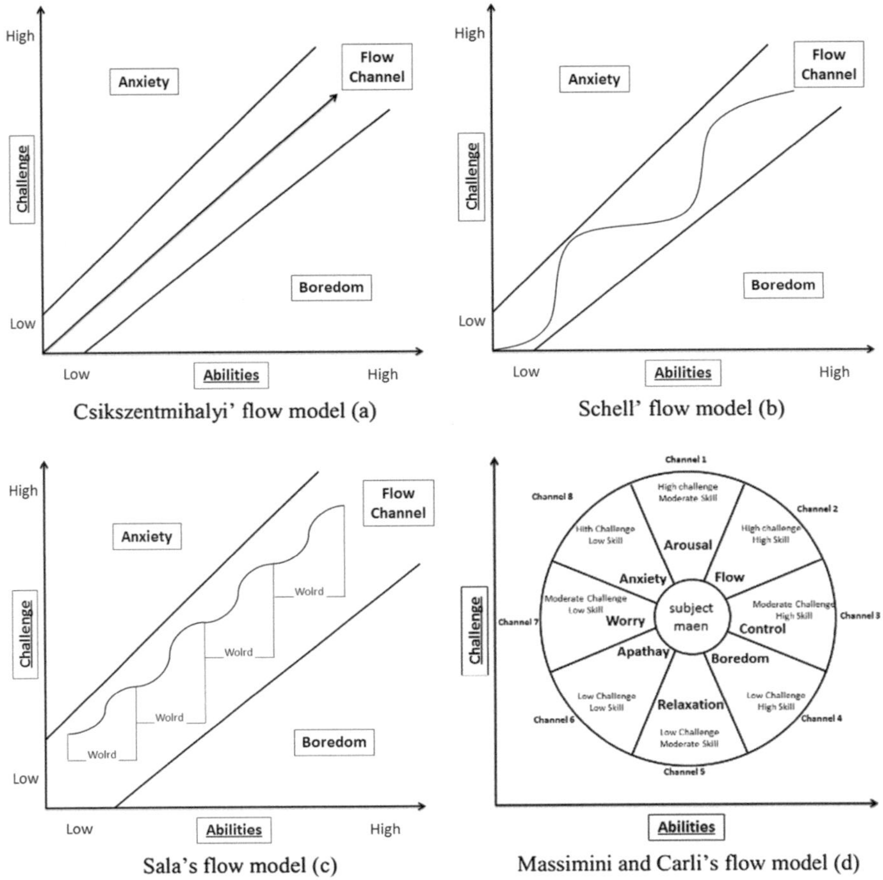

Fig. 2.2 Flow models

Nevertheless, recent studies have shown that with traditional gamification (without personalization), it can be very difficult to get students to achieve this experience. With this, the tailored gamification appears as a possible alternative to make the students reach this experience, as well as the flow experience can be seen as a way of evaluating the quality of a TGES in terms of student's enjoyment.

2.2.2 Persuasive Strategies

In general, the term persuasion is an "umbrella" term of influence, attempting to influence a person's beliefs, attitudes, intentions, motivations, or behaviors Seiter and Gass [29]. A plethora of different techniques of persuasion has been used in different contexts, for instance, in sales systems to persuade users to purchase some products or in the health and science to motivate people to practice sports [30].

Persuasion began with the Greeks, who emphasized rhetoric and elocution as the highest standard for a successful politician. The first persuasive strategy registered was the trials that were held in front of the Greek Assembly, and both the prosecution and the defense rested, as they often do today, on the persuasiveness of the speaker. Besides, over the last 20 years of research in this field, a number of PT strategies have been developed. Orji et al. [30] synthesized the studies conducted in this field in the last 20 years; during these years, some important studies were conducted. For instance, in 2003, Fogg [31] developed seven persuasive tools that can be used to persuade users in different contexts, such as marketing or health or education.

One year after the Fogg's study, Cialdini [32] also developed six persuasive principles that can be verified and applied in different contexts. More recently, Oinas-Kukkonen and Harjumaa [33] built on Fogg's strategies to develop 28 persuasive system design principles. According to Harjumaa [34], actually, these strategies are often applied in combinations when incorporated in actual software, in order to provide systems capable of persuading different users.

Persuasive strategies have a direct relationship with gamification. Gamification can be used as a persuasive strategy, that is, as a strategy to make a group of people change behavior with respect to something (e.g., the desire to study). At the same time, gamification may also make use of different persuasion strategies specific to the context and goal of gamification implementation, for instance, in tailored gamification, specific strategies can be used to make gamification more collaborative or competitive, depending on the application domain.

2.3 Computational Theories

After the international advent of gamification as a research topic, computer-based strategies began to be used as a strategy to improve the use of gamification in an educational context. Especially, computer science has been used to help gamified systems, seeking to improve the user experience on those systems. In this section, our objective will be to present general topics of computer science that relate directly to the tailored gamification, showing how these topics can contribute to provide ever better systems. We discuss specifically *(i)* artificial intelligence (AI) and *(ii)* human–computer interaction (HCI).

2.3.1 Artificial Intelligence

According to Russell and Norvig [35] in their best-seller "Artificial intelligence: a modern approach", over the years, since its inception, AI may be the field of computing that has grown the most, being discussed in many different ways. AI has been used in several lines of research, such as robotics, online sales, and of course education. The field of artificial intelligence in education (AIED) has undergone significant developments over the last 25 years [36].

In education, especially, AI has to provide important contributions related to the development of intelligent systems, for example, to automatically personalize the system design according to the student's preferences, to recommend specific contents according to the students' individual needs, or to provide interaction with students in educational systems.

Some specific AI sub-domains have been used most often, such as the data mining, that is a process of discovering patterns in large data sets involving methods at the intersection of machine learning, statistics, and database systems [37]. Similar to it, a sub-domain of data mining, text mining has also been widely used. These sub-domains of AI have been able to contribute to education in a variety of ways, such as the development of intelligent systems (e.g., intelligent tutoring systems (ITS)) that can implicitly identify different needs of students and provide specific materials for those needs.

In 2016, Pinkwart [38] discussed seven AIED challenges for the next few years: *(i)* intercultural and global dimensions of AIED; *(ii)* practical impact; *(iii)* privacy gains; *(iv)* interaction methods; *(v)* collaboration at scale; *(vi)* effectiveness in multiple; and *(vii)* role of AIED in educational technology domains. These are some of the challenges that can guide AIED work for the next few years and that support AI studies for the development of tailored gamified educational systems (TGES).

Thus, in a special way, AI can contribute to the development of TGES under two primary aspects, one related to the development of the systems and another with respect to the evaluation of this type of system. Through AI, it is possible to analyze user data produced in educational systems automatically in order to define user behavior patterns in systems (behavior with respect to gamification design), as well as to identify user preferences in order to automate the process of personalization in real time, before the actions of the users.

2.3.2 *Human–Computer Interaction*

The HCI was popularized in 1983 in the book "The Psychology of Human-Computer Interaction" of the authors Stuart Card, Thomas Moran, and Allen Newell. It refers to researches on the design and the use of computer technology, focused on the interfaces between people (users) and computers, by observing the ways in which humans interact with computers. It also designs technologies that let humans interact with computers in novel ways and presents the influence of systems design in the user satisfaction [39–41].

The Association for Computing Machinery (ACM) defines HCI as "a discipline concerned with the design, evaluation and implementation of interactive computing systems for human use and with the study of major phenomena surrounding them" [42]. CHI studies are related to many different aspects and areas. In education, especially, CHI has been used to assist in the design of systems that are capable of providing a good user experience for students, as well as for evaluating the user experience (UX) in this type of system [43–45].

In particular, gamification studies have investigated the influence of gamification on the students' experience, as well as on the relationship between the systems gamification design and the students' learning outcomes [46–49]. Studies have demonstrated a direct relationship between the good design of gamification and engagement, immersion, and learning experience of users. In other words, good gamification design can help students improve their experience in educational systems [24].

All considered, HCI can be directly related to the studies in tailored gamification for educational systems. The main connections are: the importance of using HCI principles for the design of adapted systems, which may go beyond adapting to specific interface elements, but which may occur around the entire design structure of those systems; as well as to collaborate in the evaluation of these systems in terms of the students' use experience in the TGES.

2.4 Tailored Gamification

Before we begin this session, it is important to understand the differences between three concepts that were spoken throughout this book; they are personalized gamification, customized gamification, and tailored gamification. Although there is no definitive definition of these three concepts and it is not our intention to create this definition, in this book we understand the three concepts differently.

The concept of "personalized gamification" refers to the design of systems with some sort of penalization, which can be done, for example, by changing the gamification elements of a system according to the country where the system is being used, or even change the colors of certain gamification elements according to the time at which the system is being accessed. It can be said that the term "personalized gamification" refers to a "lower level" of granularity than to the level of characterization of the system.

On the other hand, the term "tailored gamification" refers to a "deeper" type of personalization, where several characteristics of gamification design can be altered similarly and where these changes occur on the basis of different individual characteristics of each user, for example, the so-called tailored gamification occurs when, for instance, the gamification elements are changed according to different individual characteristics of each participant (e.g., student's gamer types, gender, and age) at the same time. One can say that the term "tailored gamification" refers to a "higher level" of granularity than to the level of characterization of the system.

Finally, the term "customized gamification" refers to the possibility of the student (user) changing the gamification interface design according to they own preferences. An example of what we actually call "customized gamification" is when the student can choose an avatar to represent him or her in the system (at a lower level of customization) or when the student can choose which gamification elements he or her wants to appear in your screen/interface.

Thus, in order to solve some problems related to the use of gamification in educational systems, in the last years, many studies have been highlighted the challenge of tailor the gamification according to the students' individual characteristics [50–56]. These are, in general, proposing a different solution to tailor gamified educational systems and investigating the importance of personalizing gamified educational systems based on students' characteristics.

Considered as one of the first studies to address personalization of gamification design, [57] presented a theoretical background about the relationship between various personality types and traits. Also, outlined player typologies that currently exist, and, assume that this relationship could better inform designers on a deeper level about the type of users that they are designed for.

In a more recent study, [55] developed seven different models of healthy eating behavior for the gamer types identified by *BrainHex* and explored the differences among the models, also creating two approaches for effective persuasive game design. A *one-size-fits-all* approach was proposed to motivate the majority of the population, while not demotivating any players and a personalized approach that will best motivate a particular type of gamer.

In summary, the studies related to personalized gamification are concerned in identifying students' individual characteristics and relate these preferences with the students' preferences in terms of gamification elements [30, 50, 58]. Due to being a recent area, most of the studies do not present deep results related to the students' learning outcomes on the tailored systems.

References

1. B.F. Skinner, *About Behaviorism* (Vintage, New York, 2011)
2. J.B. Watson, *Behaviorism* (Routledge, Abingdon-on-Thames, 2017)
3. B.F. Skinner, *Behavior of Organisms* (Appleton-Century-Crofts, New York, 1938)
4. J.E. Ormrod, K.M. Davis, *Human Learning* (Merrill, London, 2004)
5. L. Nagowah, S. Nagowah, A reflection on the dominant learning theories: behaviourism, cognitivism and constructivism. Int. J. Learn. **16**(2) (2009)
6. C.B. Ferster, B.F. Skinner, Schedules of reinforcement (1957)
7. J. Staddon, *The new Behaviorism* (Psychology Press, Hove, 2014)
8. G. Mandler, Origins of the cognitive (r) evolution. J. Hist. Behav. Sci. **38**(4), 339–353 (2002)
9. S.O. Lilienfeld, S.J. Lynn, L.L. Namy, N.J. Woolf, Psychology: a framework for everyday thinking (2009)
10. P.A. Ertmer, T.J. Newby, Behaviorism, cognitivism, constructivism: comparing critical features from an instructional design perspective. Perform. Improv. Q. **6**(4), 50–72 (1993)
11. P.A. Cooper, Paradigm shifts in designed instruction: from behaviorism to cognitivism to constructivism. Educ. Technol. **33**(5), 12–19 (1993)
12. J. Piaget, Piaget's theory (1970)
13. McLeod, Jean piaget's theory of cognitive development (2018)
14. J. Piaget, B. Inhelder, *The Growth of Logical Thinking from Childhood to Adolescence: An Essay on the Construction of Formal Operational Structures* (Routledge, Abingdon, 1958)

15. J. Piaget, *The Construction of Reality in the Child* (Routledge, Abingdon, 1957)
16. J.R. Anderson, L.M. Reder, H.A. Simon, K.A. Ericsson, R. Glaser, Radical constructivism and cognitive psychology. Brook. Pap. Educ. Policy **1**, 227–278 (1998)
17. L.P. Steffe, J.E. Gale, *Constructivism in Education* (Lawrence Erlbaum, Hillsdale, 1995)
18. C.T. Fosnot, *Constructivism: Theory, Perspectives, and Practice* (Teachers College Press, New York, 2013)
19. R.H. Bruning, G.J. Schraw, R.R. Ronning, *Cognitive Psychology and Instruction*. (ERIC, 1999)
20. P. Van Meter, R.J. Stevens, The role of theory in the study of peer collaboration. J. Exp. Educ. **69**(1), 113–127 (2000)
21. J.G. Greeno, A.M. Collins, L.B. Resnick et al., Cognition and learning. *Handbook of educational psychology*, vol. 77 (1996), pp 15–46
22. M. Csikszentmihalyi, *Finding Flow: The Psychology of Engagement with Everyday Life* (Basic Books, New York, 1997)
23. A. Faiola, C. Newlon, M. Pfaff, O. Smyslova, Correlating the effects of flow and telepresence in virtual worlds: Enhancing our understanding of user behavior in game-based learning. Comput. Hum. Behav. **29**(3), 1113–1121 (2013)
24. W. Admiraal, J. Huizenga, S. Akkerman, G. Ten Dam, The concept of flow in collaborative game-based learning. Comput. Hum. Behav. **27**(3), 1185–1194 (2011)
25. W.O. Santos, I.I. Bittencourt, S. Isotani, D. Dermeval, L.B. Marques, Flow theory to promote learning in educational systems: is it really relevant? Braz. J. Comput. Educ. **26**(2), 29–59 (2018)
26. J. Schell, *The Art of Game Design: A Book of Lenses* (CRC Press, Boca Raton, 2014)
27. T. Sala, Game Design Theory Applied: The Flow Channel. *Indie Dev Stories* (2010), https://goo.gl/Nh1FWq. Accessed 01 Dec 2017
28. F. Massimini, The systematic assessment of flow in daily experience, optimal experience. *Psychological Studies of Flow in Consciousness* (1988), pp. 266–287
29. R.H. Gass, J.S. Seiter, *Persuasion: Social Influence and Compliance Gaining* (Routledge, Abingdon, 2015)
30. R. Orji, R.L. Mandryk, J. Vassileva, Selecting effective strategies for tailoring persuasive health games to gamer types (2014)
31. B.J. Fogg, Persuasive technology: using computers to change what we think and do. Ubiquity **2002**(December), 5 (2002)
32. R.B. Cialdini, The science of persuasion. Sci. Am. Mind **14**(1), 70–77 (2004)
33. H. Oinas-Kukkonen, M. Harjumaa, A systematic framework for designing and evaluating persuasive systems. *Persuasive Technology* (2008), pp. 164–176
34. M. Harjumaa, K. Segerståhl, H. Oinas-Kukkonen, Understanding persuasive software functionality in practice: a field trial of polar ft60, in *Proceedings of the 4th International Conference on Persuasive Technology* (ACM, 2009), p. 2
35. S.J. Russell, P. Norvig, *Artificial Intelligence: A Modern Approach* (Pearson Education Limited, Malaysia, 2016)
36. I. Roll, R. Wylie, Evolution and revolution in artificial intelligence in education. Int. J. Artif. Intell. Educ. **26**(2), 582–599 (2016)
37. D.J. Hand, Principles of data mining. Drug Saf. **30**(7), 621–622 (2007)
38. N. Pinkwart, Another 25 years of aied? Challenges and opportunities for intelligent educational technologies of the future. Int. J. Artif. Intell. Educ. **26**(2), 771–783 (2016)
39. S.K. Card, T.P. Moran, A. Newell, The keystroke-level model for user performance time with interactive systems. Commun. ACM **23**(7), 396–410 (1980)
40. J.H. Carlisle, Evaluating the impact of office automation on top management communication, in *Proceedings of the June 7–10, 1976, National Computer Conference and Exposition* (ACM, 1976), pp. 611–616
41. G. Fischer, User modeling in human-computer interaction. User Model. User Adapt. Interact. **11**(1–2), 65–86 (2001)
42. T.T. Hewett, R. Baecker, S. Card, T. Carey, J. Gasen, M. Mantei, G. Perlman, G. Strong, W. Verplank, *ACM SIGCHI curricula for human-computer interaction* (ACM, 1992)

43. G.W. Strong, New directions in human-computer interaction: education, research, and practice. Interactions **2**(1), 69–81 (1995)
44. J. Preece, Y. Rogers, H. Sharp, *Interaction Design: Beyond Human-Computer Interaction* (Wiley, New York, 2015)
45. J. Ahn, T. Clegg, Human-computer interaction and education: Designing for technology-enhanced learning experiences. *The Wiley Handbook of Human Computer Interaction*, vol. 2 (2018), pp. 821–830
46. J. Majuri, J. Koivisto, J. Hamari, Gamification of education and learning: a review of empirical literature, in *2nd International GamiFIN Conference* (Pori, Finland, 2018), pp. 21–23
47. D. Dicheva, C. Dichev, G. Agre, G. Angelova, Gamification in education: a systematic mapping study. J. Educ. Technol. Soc. 18(3) (2015)
48. J. Hamari, J. Koivisto, H. Sarsa, Does gamification work?-a literature review of empirical studies on gamification, in *47th Hawaii international conference on system sciences (HICSS)* (IEEE, 2014), pp. 3025–3034
49. W.O. Santos, A. Toda, S. Isotani, I.I. Bittencourt, Does gamified educational systems change student's learning behaviors? A case study with postgraduate students. RENOTE **16**(2)
50. É. Lavoué, B. Monterrat, M. Desmarais, S. George, Adaptive gamification for learning environments. IEEE Trans. Learn. Technol. (2018)
51. M. Böckle, J. Novak, M. Bick, Towards adaptive gamification: a synthesis of current developments (2017)
52. F. de Vette, M. Tabak, H.J. Hermens, M. Vollenbroek, Mapping game preferences of older adults: a field study towards tailored gamified applications, in *Proceedings of the 10th Nordic Conference on Human-Computer Interaction* (ACM, 2018), pp. 93–101
53. K.M. Kapp, Choose your level: Using games and gamification to create personalized instruction. *Handbook on Personalized Learning for States, Districts, and Schools* (2016), pp. 131–143
54. J. Vassileva, Motivating participation in social computing applications: a user modeling perspective. User Model. User-Adapt. Interact. **22**(1), 177–201 (2012)
55. R. Orji, R.L. Mandryk, J. Vassileva, K.M. Gerling, Tailoring persuasive health games to gamer type, in *Proceedings of the SIGCHI Conference on Human Factors in Computing Systems* (ACM, 2013), pp. 2467–2476
56. B. Monterrat, E. Lavoué, S. George, Motivation for learning: adaptive gamification for web-based learning environments, in *6th International Conference on Computer Supported Education (CSEDU 2014)* (2014), pp. 117–125
57. L.S. Ferro, S.P. Walz, S. Greuter, Towards personalised, gamified systems: an investigation into game design, personality and player typologies, in *Proceedings of The 9th Australasian Conference on Interactive Entertainment: Matters of Life and Death* (ACM, 2013), p. 7
58. B. Monterrat, M. Desmarais, E. Lavoué, S. George, A player model for adaptive gamification in learning environments, in *International Conference on Artificial Intelligence in Education* (Springer, 2015), pp. 297–306

Chapter 3
Research Advances on Tailored Gamification

Abstract Over the previous years, mainly based on the results of experimental studies that showed that gamification can bring about poor results depending on how it was planned and applied, studies began to investigate how to improve the design of gamification systems through tailored gamification. They also present and discuss the results from the use of adapted, tailored, and customized gamified educational systems for the users. Although it is still a new research field and with few studies, some results can already be stated. In order to present and discuss recent studies in the field of tailored gamification, especially (but not exclusively) concerning the tailoring of gamification in educational systems, we present in this chapter a literature review with an overview of studies on tailored gamification, showing the main results obtained in these studies and a discussion about the conclusions presented.

3.1 Tailored Gamified Educational Technologies

The general idea of "adaptation" is young and not exclusive of gamified educational systems. Some years ago, with the advent of psychological studies that identified people's different characteristics and behaviors, many researchers, instructors, and business leaders started to identify and experiment strategies to personalize people's experience in many different kind of systems. In education, for example, for a long time studies have sought to identify how students can be better motivated by a customization of their educational environment, for example, by recommending specific tasks for each student profile, or creating groups that are most suitable for each profile.

Based on this, the first studies identified that especially in gamified environments, it is necessary to be attentive to the fact that students have different perceptions regarding games elements. The students can be motivated or unmotivated according to the elements which are present in the environment. The first studies to deal with the personalization of gamification were not in the area of education. It was only in the last four years that the earliest studies dealing specifically with the personalization of gamification into gamified educational systems began to emerge, generally using the approach proposed for other areas and adapting it to education.

W. Oliveira and I. I. Bittencourt, *Tailored Gamification to Educational Technologies*,
https://doi.org/10.1007/978-981-32-9812-5_3

The studies that deal with the personalization of gamification generally focus on three aspects as a basis for personalization: user's gamer types, gender, and age. Especially when it comes to the TGES, the vast majority of studies dealt with personalization based on the student's gamer type only, in detriment to approaches that dealt with personalization based on other aspects. Most of the studies also dealt with personalization based only on the gamification design, independent of the pedagogical design of the system.

3.1.1 Tailored Educational Technologies Based on Students' Characteristics

Considered as one of the first studies to address personalization of gamification design, Ferro et al. [1] presented a theoretical background about the relationship between various personality types and traits. They also outlined player typologies that actually exist and assumed that this relationship could better provide for the designers a deeper level about the type of users that they are designing for [1].

In their study, they identified that game elements and mechanics may provide a dynamic toolbox to better inform the design of gamified systems and specifically target users in a more intrinsically engaging and motivating way. The authors clarify that their results are an initial step toward personalizing gamified systems. However, they argue the study requires further research and validation, as well as a deeper investigation into not only the relationship between player typologies and personality traits and types but also on the relation between game elements and mechanics.

The study conducted by Ferro and his colleagues is important because it provides an initial structure to personalize a different kind of gamified system, as well to highlight if the gamified system that uses the same gamification elements to both students can frustrate or demotivate them. The results also emphasize the importance of personalizing these gamified systems based on the user's gamer type. However, the study is merely theoretical and do not provide any evaluation to the proposal, as highlighted by the authors of the study.

In order to give another important step in tailoring of gamified environments, Orji et al. [2] pointed that most games and gamified environments adopt a "one-size-fits-all" approach to engagement in their design. This is a bad design approach because a motivational approach that works for one individual may actually demotivate the desired behavior in others [3].

Orji and her colleagues conducted a large-scale study on 1108 gamers, which examined the efficiency of ten persuasive strategies, and the receptiveness of seven gamer types identified by *BrianHex* player model [4] to the techniques most commonly used. They also developed models showing the receptiveness of the gamer types to the ten strategies and created persuasive profiles, which is a list of strategies that can be employed to motivate behavior for each gamer type [3].

In another study, Orji et al. [3] developed seven different models of healthy eating behaviors for the gamer types identified by *BrainHex* and explored the differences between the models, also creating two approaches for effective persuasive game design. A "one-size-fits-all" approach was proposed to motivate the majority of the population, while not demotivating any players. A personalized approach that can be best used to motivate a particular type of gamer was also proposed.

The studies conducted by Orji and her colleagues are important because they highlight the importance of tailoring gamified systems based on gamer types. They also provide a relationship between better persuasive strategies to motivate each gamer type and a guideline to design this kind of system. However, such studies were conducted in the field of health science, which shows a gap in other fields, such as education.

Magerko et al. [5] presented an approach for methodically identifying the possible adaptations a game can take and mapping those adaptations to the learner's needs. They describe a prototype mini-game, called S.C.R.U.B., which intelligently adapts its gameplay based on an individual player's learning style. This study addresses three different gamer types (Explorer, Achiever, and Winner) based on Bartle's player model. In their study, the game experience was first analyzed to identify the different features that make up the gameplay, the interface, and the knowledge presented to the player (e.g., having a high score, the visualization of text-based facts, and having a time limit). It ended up with six initial adaptive features of particular importance to Explorers, Achievers, or Winners.

The study conducted by Magerko et al. [5] gave an important initial contribution to the game design field, especially because it provided an association among game feature preferences for three different gamer types. However, the study was not conducted using a complete player type, like *BrainHex*, it also did not do an association between player types and game mechanics or persuasive technologies and did not conduct a deep evaluation in terms of user's experience, for instance, concentration, engagement, and others. Hence, there is an open space to conduct studies with these characteristics in domains such as gamified educational systems.

Jovanovic et al. [6] proposed an approach in order to identify and design profiles-based user interfaces for educational games. The proposed approach was based on framing games as educational tools incorporating fun and learning through motivation as the key "ingredient" in the learning process, as well as "multimodal" interaction as the means for conveying educational material. The authors stress that, to date, there is no common standard to design this kind of games and individual solutions are usually carried out by an ad hoc process. In their study, it is also possible to see an example of a developed game interface based on the model proposed.

In this study, Jovanovic et al. [6] proposed a framework capable of helping game designers to tailor educational games interface. The study, nevertheless, did not present concerns about the analysis of the student's gamer type, for instance, how to tailor the game interface based on students' gamer types or evaluate the game tailored in comparison with the same game without personalization.

Heeter et al. [7] considered whether and how eight different and modern games design Explorers, Achievers, and Self-validators profiles and discuss implications for entertainment and learning game design and research. Seven of the eight different games analyzed served either the Explorer or Achiever player types. The Self-validators player types were partially organized in some Achiever-oriented games through user-selectable difficulty [7]. A design that considers all three types would encourage the inclusion of features that enable players to optimize their preferred style of play [7].

The study executed by Heeter et al. [7] showed that it is important to tailor educational games based on student's gamer types, and the results show that tailored games can better increase the students' motivation and learning. This study emphasizes the importance in conducting researches also aiming to tailor gamified educational systems.

Thammanichanon and Kotrajaras [8] pointed in their study that Player Archetype Change Management (PACM) system that is a drama management system changes the story of role playing games according to a specific player model monitored during gameplay. Authors gave each of his stories a matching player model. While a player plays the game, PACM selects the story that most matches the current player model. However, players may not agree with a model defined for a story by its author [8].

In their study, the authors present a technique for adjusting the player model of each story in PACM using observed data from players and to provide the system with a more reliable player model for future playing sessions. On one hand, the study of Thammanichanon and Kotrajaras [8] provided for our understanding on the importance of tailoring educational environments based on the students' preferences. On the other hand, the study is limited in terms of a proposal to tailor this kind of environment, without presenting the player model or the evaluation used during the study conduction [8]. The study is also quite limited in terms of comprehensiveness, and it presents an open gap to conduct new studies in this field.

Sajjadi et al. [9] proposed a model for a richer dynamic adaptation, in which several aspects are taken into account in order to provide a more personalized gaming experience to sustain the engagement of the players to the game. The model allows an adaptation in an educational game based on different aspects and different moments, in order to provide a rich personalized experience, to sustain the engagement of the learner, and thus providing a more suitable frame for the flow experience [9].

On the study made by Sajjadi and their colleagues, they take important points into account, such as the engagement of the learning of the player, as well as the evaluation of whether the frame is suitable for the flow experience on the users. The study, however, did not provide concerns about the use of the player model and the relationship between the users' gamer type and their preferences on game elements. The study was conducted in the field of game design with open space to conduct similar studies in similar areas, such as gamified educational systems.

Monterrat et al. [10] proposed a complementary player model to existing learner models, aiming to predict to which game mechanics the user is responsive, in order to adapt the gamified features of the system [10]. The authors designed a gamification layer composed of gaming features, a player model, and an adaptation engine for selecting the features for the users.

In the framework proposed by Monterrat and his colleagues, the gaming features are represented by a vector based on the classification of Ferro et al. [1], with values between 0 and 1. For instance, the ranking vector could be (dominant 1, humanist 0.7, objectivist 0.3, creative 0, inquisitive 0). The users are represented in the same way. Indeed, the users are generally interested in more than one game mechanic. The study also proposed an adaptive engine for select the features for the users.

The study conducted by Monterrat et al. [10] was important in order to start the investigation about tailoring educational systems based on gamer types in the field of education. However, the study conducted by Monterrat and his colleagues is an initial research and do not provide concerns about the player model used to conduct the research, as well as it do not present the implementation or evaluation of the proposal.

In order to deepen the aforementioned research, in another study Monterrat et al. [11] presents an adaptive generic gamification system that can be plugged on various learning environments. The architecture of the proposed system was based on the separation between the control of the pedagogical elements and the control of the game elements.

In his proposal, the adaptation of the system happens after the student starts to use the system, and basically, when a new user registers in the learning system, the values of the motivational factors are started for the user according to their data. During the use of the learning system, the values change in according to the user's interactions in the system. If the users disable some item in the system, the values for the corresponding gamer types will decrease; if users interact often with a gaming feature, their values for the corresponding player types increase [11].

Moreover, taken the study conducted by Monterrat et al. [11] to provide a gamification system that can be plugged on various learning environments, the adaptation of the system happens only after the student uses it sometimes, first identifying the students to a state of demotivation, to change the gamification model in the system, and it could harm the user's experience in the system.

Furthermore, the study conducted by Monterrat and his colleagues used the initial player model proposed by Ferro et al. [1], which considers only a few number of player types, and do not provide empirical validation. At the same time, they do not consider more recent and robust player models, such as *BrainHex*, that contemplate seven different gamer types and were empirically evaluated.

Monterrat and his colleagues also presented, in another study (Monterrat et al. [12]), a generic/adaptive gamification system that can be plugged on different educational systems. The system will be automatically tailored based on an interaction analysis. In this specific study, they also presented an architecture for the proposed system in order to support the generic game elements [12].

Monterrat and his colleagues provide a generic architecture that can be used to adapt the gamification in different kinds of system, apart from the pedagogical design. This study has not presented concerns in terms of choice of player profiles, as well as did not provide information about the architecture evaluation in terms of students engagement or students' learning during their experience using the personalized system based on the proposed architecture.

In a more recent study from the same research group, Monterrat et al. [13] presented a generic and adaptive gamification system that can also be plugged on general learning systems. In this proposal, the game elements can be automatically adapted, based on an analysis of the user's interaction traces. The system architecture proposed is based on the separation between the control of the pedagogical elements and the control of the game elements [12, 13]. To support the adaptability of the game elements, the authors refer to a user model based on a list of player types, the user model has been initialized thanks to the traces of interactions and finally was used to predict which game feature will be relevant for the user [12, 13].

In this study, Monterrat and his colleagues also presented their architecture to adapt gamification systems, taking into account the students' gamer type, and using the *BrainHex* player model to classify them. The purpose was to provide a tailored gamified system based on the students' game preferences. In this study, however, Monterrat and his colleagues have not presented concerns about the architecture evaluation, and its applicability to tailor the gamification design of gamified educational systems.

Monterrat et al. [13] also present a model to tailor gamification features according to a player profile of the learners. Two versions of this model were evaluated within a gamified online learning environment, and the first version comes from expert's judgment, and the second one is induced from empirical data [13].

In this specific study, Monterrat and his colleagues also evaluated the two versions of its system (tailored and counter-tailored system). The evaluation was conducted in two steps, the first by specialists, and the second using empirical data. This study did not present concerns regarding the students' receptiveness of the system, or the students' learning, in the comparison between the tailored and the counter-tailored system. It highlights the importance of conducting deeper studies in terms to comparatively evaluation between tailored and counter-tailored systems.

Monterrat et al. [13] presented a model to tailor the gamification features according to the student's gamer type. In their study, two versions of the model were evaluated within a gamified online learning environment. The first version comes from experts' judgment, and the second one is induced from empirical data [13]. The experiments conducted confirmed that the first version can be efficient to predict the players' preferences among the gamification features. The approach was so that the adaptive interface of the learning environment would rely on two separate engines developed independently, one for the didactic content adaptation and the other for the gamification adaptation [13].

They also developed a model that estimates the preference for a feature by a weighted sum of personality traits, which bears similarities to existing learner models that predict students success based on a linear or boolean combination of skills. In the same study, two experiments were conducted, the first experiment in order to associate the player type (using *BrainHex* player model) with the game features preferences (five different game features were used: Stars, Leader, Board, Tips, Walker, and Timer). As in experiment one, they filled in the *BrainHex* questionnaire, answering game feature assessment questions. The members of the first group were provided with the two game features that best matched their profile, and the members of the second group, with the two features that worse matched their profile.

In this study, the authors provided a strong contribution to the field of user modeling based on gamer types, especially because Monterrat and his colleagues take into account the *BrainHex* player model and their preferences about the gamification style in the educational system. The study, however, is limited in terms of gamification elements, addressing about only five different game features (Stars, Leader board, Tips, Walker, and Timer), without taking into account other important game features, as well as forgetting to associate these game features with their respective persuasive technology, and evaluate the system tailored in terms of students' receptiveness.

Torrente et al. [14] explored the potential impact of a semi-automatic adaptation of game interfaces design as a way to facilitate accessible game development (and thus trim the cost down). The authors proposed a game interface model optimized for "point-and-click" adventure games, a popular genre among serious games that were used to perform different semi-automatic adaptations in a game [14]. The authors had tested the resulting adapted game with end users with specific disability profiles. The tests discovered that the automatic adaptations produced usable games that retained part of their attractiveness, although different usability issues had a negative impact on the user's experience [14].

The study conducted by Torrente et al. [14] was an important step to emphasize the need to tailor game interface, as well as gamified systems interface, in order to increase the player's experience. However, the study is focused on the field of serious game, without comprehensiveness to the field of educational environments, and provides an evaluation just in the scope of the game interface. The study makes it clear the importance to conduct similar studies in another field and evaluate the solutions in different terms.

Gil et al. [15] presented a preliminary user study in an e-learning environment aimed to adapt and validate generic mechanics and player types proposed in the gamification literature. They incorporated well-known gamification mechanics into a number of learning activities, implementing them as functionalities of an e-learning system and investigating the learning effectiveness of the proposed mechanics, as well the relations between the mechanics and their assumed player types. In summary, the study of Gil et al. [15] had at first validated gamification mechanics and player types in education and identified if the gamification mechanics really corresponded to the students' inferred player types.

This study also provided an important initial step in order to associate gamification mechanics and player types, showing that students are differently engaged in gamified educational systems according to their gamer type. However, the study did not provide resources so that gamification designers could start to design systems tailored based on the students' gamer types, further underlining the importance in conducting deeper studies in order to provide ways for professionals from industry and academy to be able to design educational system personalized according to their users' gamer type.

Manero et al. [16] developed a tool to gamers to classify according to their preferences and habits, classifying the participants into four "clusters" (gamer types), allowing an easy results interpretation. The gamer types are: (1) Full gamers, covering individuals that play all kinds of games with a high frequency; (2) Hardcore gamers, playing mostly first-person shooters and sport games; (3) Casual gamers, playing moderately musical, social and thinking games; and (4) Non-gamers, who do not usually play games of any kind. The instrument may have been used in psychology and behavioral sciences, as there is evidence suggesting that attitudes toward gaming affect personal attitudes and behavior [16].

The study performed by Manero et al. [16] is a very young study highlighting the importance in understanding the relationship between gamer types and their preferences in terms of systems' usability, as well as to provide tailored system to each gamer profile, especially in educational domains, such as educational games, or gamified educational systems.

Knutas et al. [17] presented in their study, conducted in 2016, evidence-based method and a case study where interaction analysis and *k-means* clustering were used to create gamification preference profiles; these profiles can be used to create adaptive gamification approach for online learning or collaborative learning environments, improving static gamification designs [17].

This study helps gamification designers to tailor educational systems creating adaptive gamification models to improve the students' learning. This study, however, is limited in terms of providing a practical structure to design gamified educational systems personalized based on gamer types, making it clear the importance to provide resources so that gamification designer can create TGES based on students' preferences or students' gamer types, such as architectures and frameworks to facilitate the tailoring process.

Silpasuwanchai et al. [18] proposed a comprehensive framework of engagement in gamification for learning. The framework sketches out the connections among gamification strategies, dimensions of engagement and the ultimate learning outcome [18]. The framework also provides an in-depth understanding of the mechanism of gamification for learning and can serve as a theoretical foundation for future research and design [18].

In this study, Silpasuwanchai and their colleagues provided a relationship between gamification strategies and dimensions of engagement toward learning, constructing an important framework for the community to understand. The study provides the understanding that specific game design elements can help a more specific player; however, it did not provide steps to help gamification designers to tailor educational gamified systems according to students' gamer types.

Challco et al. [19] proposed an ontological model for the formal systematization and representation of knowledge, describing the concepts of gamification theory and its use as a persuasive technology (PT) in collaborative learning scenarios (CLS). The model of Challco and his colleagues enabled the creation of intelligent educational systems that can personalize and apply the gamification techniques in group learning contexts in which the scripted collaboration decreases the motivation and engagement of students [19]. The approach proposed formalize a connection of concepts from theories and models to design PT in order to specify gamified CLS scripts, to induce students to willingly follow an intended learning behavior [19]. They also presented a case study that showed how the proposed approach could be used by in an intelligent theory-aware system to build better personalized gamified CLS.

The work developed by Challco and his colleagues in 2016 is a recent study providing an important contribution for gamification designers to tailor gamified educational environments based on the specific group of students in CL scenarios, connecting PT strategies and gamification elements in CL scenarios, aiming to better tailor gamified CL scenarios and increase the students learning. The study by Challco et al. [19] did not have concerns in terms of tailoring the system based on students' gamer types or evaluating the system in terms of students' emotions during their experience using the personalized system.

In more recent studies, different researchers continue to propose computational approaches in order to personalize the gamified educational systems according to the students' characteristics. In 2017, Knutas and his colleagues [20] proposed an approach for personalizing gamification to the needs of each individual person in computer-supported CLS and a method for translating gamification "rulesets" to machine-readable classifier algorithm using the algorithm "CN2" and a framework for connecting the produced algorithm to collaborative software. In this same study, they also presented an example software for personalized gamification that was produced by applying the process.

In 2018, [21] and his colleagues published another study proposing a machine learning algorithm-based personalized content selection and a process for creating personalized designs that allow automating a part of the implementation. The process is based on Deterding's framework for gameful design. In this study, they used the gamification user type Hexad for personalization and the heuristics for effective design of gamification for overall design.

Also in 2018, Lopez and Tucker [22] proposed a machine learning-based approach that uses task information and an individual's facial expression data recognition aiming to predict the student's performance on a specific gamified activity, with a adaptive-individual-activity model updated every time from an individual acquired characteristic. The findings support the use of adaptive models that dynamically update the training data set and consider task information and individuals' facial expression data [22].

In view of the studies presented in this chapter, it is possible to draw some important conclusions for the future of the area. When we read the studies, two things are clear: The first is that it is a new area, with the main studies being carried out in the last 5 years, usually based on theoretical or empirical studies from other areas such as psychology. The second thing that is clear when we read the studies is that despite the interesting advances made over the last few years, many things still need to be done, both in providing better ways of personalizing the gamified educational systems and in identifying whether these kinds of systems are capable of improving students' experiences.

References

1. L.S. Ferro, S.P. Walz, S. Greuter, Towards personalised, gamified systems: an investigation into game design, personality and player typologies, in *Proceedings of The 9th Australasian Conference on Interactive Entertainment: Matters of Life and Death* (ACM, 2013), p. 7
2. R. Orji, R.L. Mandryk, J. Vassileva, K.M. Gerling, Tailoring persuasive health games to gamer type, in *Proceedings of the SIGCHI Conference on Human Factors in Computing Systems* (ACM, 2013), pp. 2467–2476
3. R. Orji, R.L. Mandryk, J. Vassileva, Selecting effective strategies for tailoring persuasive health games to gamer types (2014)
4. L.E. Nacke, C. Bateman, R.L. Mandryk, Brainhex: a neurobiological gamer typology survey. Entertain. Comput. **5**(1), 55–62 (2014)
5. B. Magerko, C. Heeter, J. Fitzgerald, B. Medler, Intelligent adaptation of digital game-based learning, in *Proceedings of the 2008 Conference on Future Play: Research, Play, Share* (ACM, 2008), pp. 200–203
6. M. Jovanovic, D. Starcevic, V. Stavljanin, M. Minovic, Educational games design issues: motivation and multimodal interaction, in *Emerging Technologies and Information Systems for the Knowledge Society* (2008), pp. 215–224
7. C. Heeter, B. Magerko, B. Medler, J. Fitzgerald, Game design and the challenge-avoiding, self-validator player type. Int. J. Gaming Comput. Mediat. Simul. (IJGCMS) **1**(3), 53–67 (2009)
8. N. Thammanichanon, V. Kotrajaras, Automatically adjusting player models for given stories in role-playing games
9. P. Sajjadi, F. Van Broeckhoven, O. De Troyer, Dynamically adaptive educational games: a new perspective, in *International Conference on Serious Games* (Springer, 2014), pp. 71–76
10. B. Monterrat, É. Lavoué, S. George, Toward an adaptive gamification system for learning environments, in *International Conference on Computer Supported Education* (Springer, 2014), pp. 115–129
11. B. Monterrat, É. Lavoué, S. George, A framework to adapt gamification in learning environments, in *European Conference on Technology Enhanced Learning* (Springer, 2014), pp. 578–579
12. B. Monterrat, E. Lavoué, S. George, Motivation for learning: adaptive gamification for web-based learning environments, in *6th International Conference on Computer Supported Education (CSEDU 2014)* (2014), pp. 117–125
13. B. Monterrat, M. Desmarais, E. Lavoué, S. George, A player model for adaptive gamification in learning environments, in *International Conference on Artificial Intelligence in Education* (Springer, 2015), pp. 297–306
14. J. Torrente, M. Freire, P. Moreno-Ger, B. Fernández-Manjón, Evaluation of semi-automatically generated accessible interfaces for educational games. Comput. Educ. **83**, 103–117 (2015)
15. B. Gil, I. Cantador, A. Marczewski, Validating gamification mechanics and player types in an e-learning environment, in *Design for Teaching and Learning in a Networked World* (Springer, 2015), pp. 568–572
16. B. Manero, J. Torrente, M. Freire, B. Fernández-Manjón, An instrument to build a gamer clustering framework according to gaming preferences and habits. Comput. Hum. Behav. **62**, 353–363 (2016)
17. A. Knutas, J. Ikonen, D. Maggiorini, L. Ripamonti, J. Porras, Creating student interaction profiles for adaptive collaboration gamification design. Int. J. Hum. Cap. Inf. Technol. Prof. (IJHCITP) **7**(3), 47–62 (2016)
18. C. Silpasuwanchai, X. Ma, H. Shigemasu, X. Ren, Developing a comprehensive engagement framework of gamification for reflective learning, in *Proceedings of the 2016 ACM Conference on Designing Interactive Systems* (ACM, 2016), pp. 459–472
19. G.C. Challco, D.A. Moreira, I.I. Bittencourt, R. Mizoguchi, S. Isotani, Personalization of gamification in collaborative learning contexts using ontologies. IEEE Lat. Am. Trans. **13**(6), 1995–2002 (2015)

20. A. Knutas, R. van Roy, T. Hynninen, M. Granato, J. Kasurinen, J. Ikonen, Profile-based algorithm for personalized gamification in computer-supported collaborative learning environments, in *GHITALY@ CHItaly* (2017)
21. A. Knutas, R. van Roy, T. Hynninen, M. Granato, J. Kasurinen, J. Ikonen, A process for designing algorithm-based personalized gamification. Multimed. Tools Appl. 1–20 (2018)
22. C. Lopez, C. Tucker, Towards personalized adaptive gamification: a machine learning model for predicting performance. IEEE Trans. Games (2018)

Chapter 4
Tailoring Gamified Educational Technologies

Abstract Despite recent studies highlighting the importance of adapting educational systems, there is a lack of systematic structures that assist developers, designers, and other stakeholders in the development of TGES according to students' characteristics. Therefore, in this chapter, we draw on recent studies on persuaded technologies and personalized gamification to propose a systematic approach to tailor gamified educational systems based on student's gamer types (considering the seven *BrainHex* gamer types). Through the proposed approach, it is possible to provide an adapted gamification design of any type of educational technology, regardless of the pedagogical design of the technology.

4.1 Strategies to Tailor Gamified Educational Technologies

In recent years, studies on tailored gamification have grown, and as discussed in the previous chapters, they have also sought different alternatives for personalized gamified systems (especially gamified educational systems). Among the studied approaches are: the Personalization based on the gamer types, user's gender, or even based on the users' age. With the objective of demonstrating a possibility for the Personalization of gamified educational systems, as well as presenting a practical approach, capable of being used by Gamification Designer, Pedagogues, and Programmers in personalizing gamified educational systems, we will present in this chapter an approach to personalize this kind of systems based on player types. The approach follows a number of psychological, educational, and computational aspects already discussed in the earlier chapters of this book.

4.1.1 An Approach to Tailor Gamified Educational Technologies Based on Students' Gamer Types

The approach was proposed based on Orji's guideline [1, 2]. Orji's guideline is a systematic structure that provides the best PT strategies for each *BrainHex* gamer

W. Oliveira and I. I. Bittencourt, *Tailored Gamification to Educational Technologies*,
https://doi.org/10.1007/978-981-32-9812-5_4

Table 4.1 PT strategies to BrainHex gamer types by Orji et al. [2]

Best strategies			
Gamer type	Best first strategy	Best second strategy	Best third strategy
Achiever	Cooperation	Reward	Self-monitoring and Suggestion
Conqueror	Competition and Comparison	Simulation	Personalization
Daredevil	Simulation	–	–
Mastermind	Self-monitoring and Suggestion	Competition and Comparison	Personalization
Seeker	Customization	Personalization	Competition and Comparison
Socializer	Cooperation	Competition and Comparison	–
Survivor	Self-monitoring and Suggestion	Competition and Comparison	–

type and the game mechanics associated with each PT strategy addressed. In other words, these are the persuasive strategies which best motivate each gamer type and its game mechanics. The best persuasive strategies associated with each gamer type addressed are presented in Table 4.1, and the association between each PT strategy and its game mechanics will be presented in Table 4.2. Figure 4.1 summarizes the best PT strategy to each gamer type and the game mechanics present in each PT strategy.

Orji's guidelines provide an important step to tailor gamified systems associating the best PT strategies to each gamer type. However, the guideline does not provide a systematic structure to tailor the systems, making it difficult to understand and identify which are the specific game design elements that should be used in the gamified system to motivate the students based on their gamer type and how to design or modify preexisting systems based on the guidelines.

Based on Orji's guideline, as well as the popular literature about gamification and game design (e.g., Hamari et al. [3], Nah et al. [4], Schuytema [5], Dicheva and Dichev [6], and Fullerton [7]), we have created a systematic structure associating the gamification elements to each persuasive strategy addressed in Orji's guideline and also, as a consequence, associating the best game design elements and gamification elements to each gamer type (see Table 4.3).

The proposal consists of an approach design that can be used to implement gamified educational systems independent of its pedagogical model. The implementation of our proposal happens as a service system, using students' data (initial students' data should be required when the student begins to use the system) to identify the students' gamer type (through the *BrainHex* questionnaire). The proposed solution must provide a registration system for the participant, and the registration must pro-

Table 4.2 PT strategies associated with the game mechanics by Orji et al. [2]

Strategies and game mechanics

Strategies	Game mechanics	Explanation
Praise	Level	Level as a sign of a good job can serve as praise for actions. Players can level up and gain new abilities
	Pride	Feeling of joy and fulfillment after accomplishment
Cooperation	Communal Discovery	The community must work together to overcome obstacles, individual effort is undermined
	Social fabric of the games	People grow closer after playing together; people will play together to make friends
	Viral game mechanics	Game elements that are more enjoyable or only accessible with others will make people want to cooperate
	Companionship gaming	Cross-platform gaming can be used to increase the opportunity for many players to play together
Competition and Comparison	Status	Rank players to force them to compare with each other and therefore compete
	Envy	Striving for what other players have will increase Competition and Comparison
	Countdown	Players only get a limited amount of time to complete challenge
	Leaderboard	Displaying high scores in Leaderboards will introduce Competition and Comparison
Reward	Physical goods	Distributing physical goods to reward players might lead to increased performance especially if the physical good appeals to players but it might also divert the intention of performing the task
	Virtual items	Distributing virtual items to reward players. This may be counterproductive
	Reward schedules	Variable and fixed reward intervals to encourage performance
	Lottery	Give players opportunity of winning stuff
	Free lunch	Give players free gifts
	Points	Success measurement on in-game actions
	Bonuses	In-game reward for overcoming challenges to reinforce desired behavior, e.g., combos
Simulation	Appointments	Fixed in-game appointments to make players return at certain times
	Leaderboards	Leaderboards to display and project high scores over time
	Achievements	Virtual/physical representation of accomplishment; achievements can be broken and tied to tasks, it can also be projected

(continued)

Table 4.2 (continued)

Strategies and game mechanics		
	Status	Player rank or level to show and project a link between behavior and outcome
	Epic meaning	Having something great as a background story to give meaning to in-game actions. The story could link behavioral outcomes to the players' actions
	Behavior momentum	Players keep going on because they feel what they are doing is valuable. Projected behavior outcome over a longer period will increase value and reinforce behavior
	Urgent optimism	High self-motivation, players want to work on issues instantly with the belief that they will succeed.
	Blissful productivity	Players work hard within game if actions are meaningful
Personalization	Cascading info. theory	Gradually introducing players to the game will create a sense of personal relevance
	Epic meaning	Having something epic as a background story to give meaning to in-game actions. The story can be tailored to each player using various characteristics e.g., gender
	Privacy	Certain information is shared, certain information is kept private for the user alone
Customization	Shell game	Illusion of choice to guide the player to the desired outcome will create a sense of Customization
	Discovery	Giving players opportunity to explore and find new things makes players fill a sense of control and autonomy associated with Customization
	Epic meaning	Having something epic as background story to give meaning to in-game actions
Self-monitoring and Suggestion	Quest	Displaying tasks that the player must complete help the player monitor his performance and progress
	Achievement	Virtual/physical representation of accomplishment enables players to monitor progress
	Level	Players receive Points for actions to show performance and progress, and they can level up and gain new abilities
	Loss aversion	Not punishing the player as long as the desired behavior is shown (but not rewarding either)
	Repeat simple action	Players enjoy repeating simple in-game actions

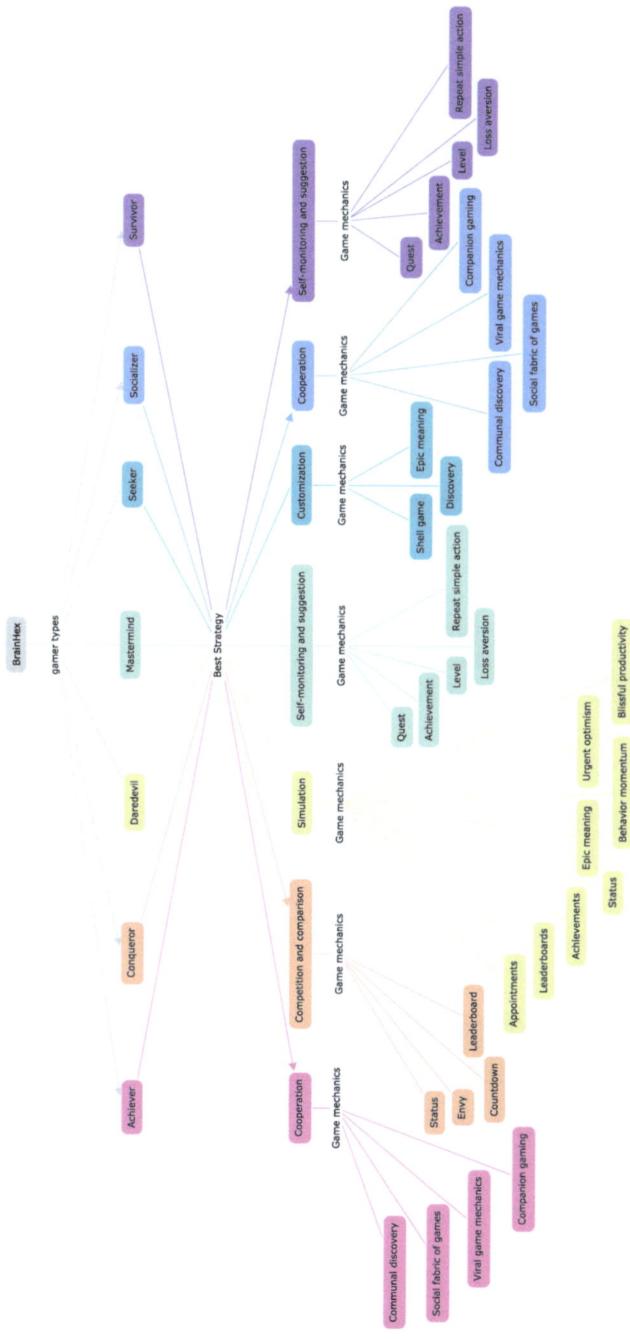

Fig. 4.1 Gamer types associated with persuasive strategies and game mechanics

Table 4.3 Gamer types and game design elements

Gamer types	Gamification elements
Achiever	Team missions
	Points
	Badges
	Trophies
	Surprise Rewards
Conqueror	Ranking
	Leaderboard
	Limited time
	Timeline
	Badges
	Adapted history according to the student's gender
Daredevil	Ranking
	Leaderboard
	Progress bar
	General history
Mastermind	Progress bar
	Points
	Badges
	Ranking
	Leaderboard
	Limited time/ Timing
	Adapted history according to the student's gender
Seeker	Choose the prizes
	Adapted history according to the student's gender
	Ranking
	Leaderboard
	Limited time/ Timing
Socializer	Team missions
	Ranking
	Leaderboard
	Comparison
Survivor	Progress bar
	Points
	Ranking
	Leaderboard
	Limited time/ Timing

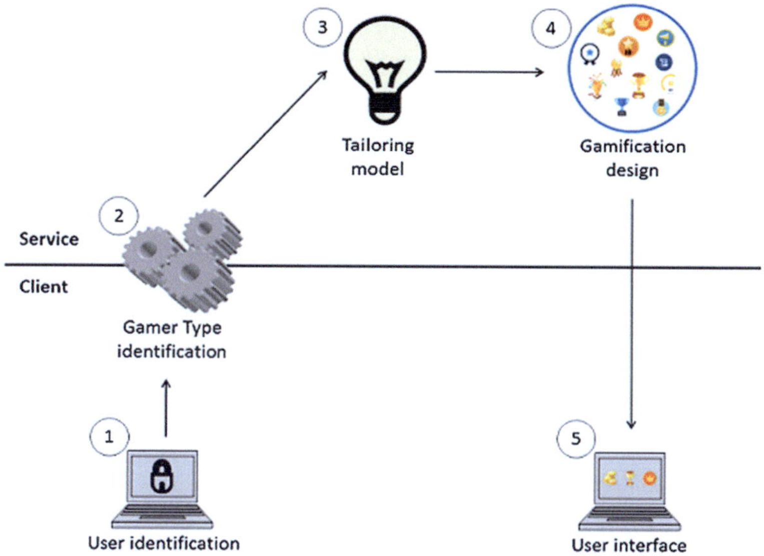

Fig. 4.2 Architectural design

vide options for the students to insert their personal data (according to the general specifications of the system).

The system needs to provide a way to identify the student's gamer type (*BrainHex* questionnaire). After the student's gamer type identification, the implemented system based on our approach design will be capable of providing a gamification system (graphical interface) tailored using as basis the student' gamer type. Basically, the general architecture is composed of five different moments. Figure 4.2 synthesizes this structure:

1. **User's identification**: In the first moment, the system must provide options for the students to create an account in the system and provide basic information, such as login, password, email, and others (according to the default system specifications). These data are important to hereafter associate the student with their gamer type. In the case of preexisting systems (edited by the proposed structure), the basic information previously obtained can be used.
2. **Gamer type identification**: The gamer type identification consists of a semi-automatic process, based on the BrainHex player model. At the same moment of the user's identification, the system should provide the BrainHex questionnaire to the students. After the student completes the questionnaire, the system should process the student's answers, identify the student's gamer type, and begin to provide a system tailored on the student's gamer type. In the case of preexisting systems (edited by the proposed architectural design), the system can provide the BrainHex questionnaire after the student logs in the system and associate their personal data and their gamer type.

3. **Tailoring process**: The tailoring is the main step of the process. In general, the tailoring model is responsible for the identification of the student's gamer type, making the game design elements available on the system, and associating algorithmically the correct game design elements to each student's gamer type, based on the structure previously defined.
4. **Gamification design**: The gamification design is the system model, responsible for generating the student's graphical interface with the best game design elements associated with their gamer type, based on the tailoring model process before its execution.
5. **User's interface**: The user's interface represents the system's output and is responsible for providing the students with the game elements design associated with their player type, generated by the gamification design model.

The system structure is composed of three different parts: front-end, back-end, and satellite. The front-end is responsible for the user's graphical interface (input and output), the back-end is responsible for the gamification system processing (Tailor Model), and finally, the satellite is an external component, using the elements from the third part (original gamified system). Figure 4.3 presents a high-level diagram of components.

The system begins with the *BrainHex* questionnaire component (input component), responsible for identifying the student's gamer type. The student's gamer type is used by the User Control component. The User Control component uses the data allowed by the User Repository component to associate the student's data with the gamer type. The Tailor Model component (main system component) uses the student's data (including the student's gamer type) and the system game design elements, associating the best gamification elements to each gamer type and creating the tailored user's graphical interface. The generated interface component (tailored interface) presents the tailored system based on the student gamer type previously

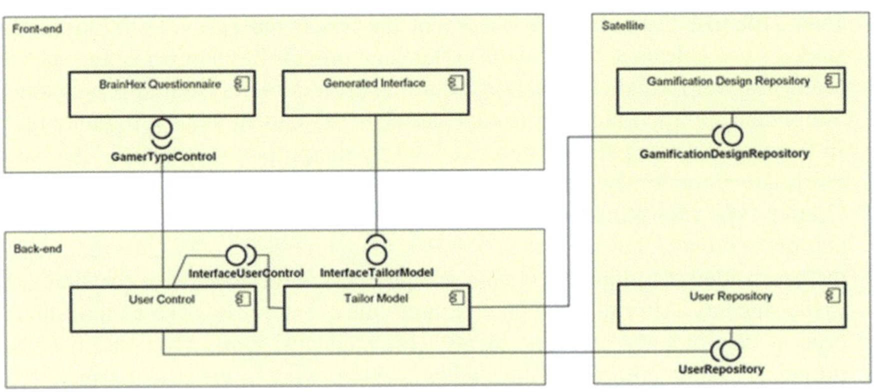

Fig. 4.3 Architectural design component diagram

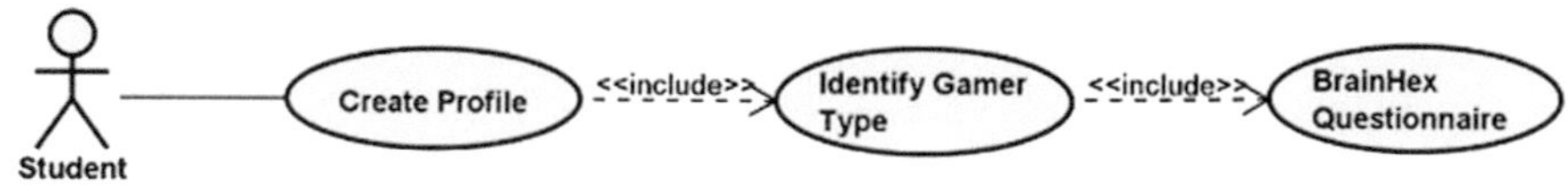

Fig. 4.4 Tailor system use case (Student actor)

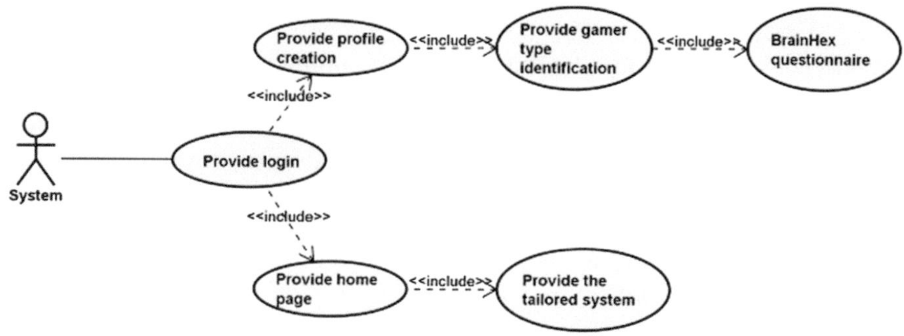

Fig. 4.5 Tailor system use case (System actor)

created. Figure 4.5 presents a use case based on the system implementation design, and Fig. 4.5 presents a use case based on the student as an user.

To create an account and identify the student's gamer type, the default process is shown on the use case presented in Fig. 4.4, based on the student's (client) perspective. Initially, the student should create their account (create a profile), with their basic information. The created profile includes the gamer type identification through the *BrainHex* questionnaire.

At the same time, with the view based on the system (author), as showed in Fig. 4.5, for the student's first login, the system provides a home page with options for the students to create their profile (first access), or log into the system. In the first case, the system provides options for the students to create their profile and identify their gamer type through the *BrainHex* questionnaire. After this process, the student can use the tailored system, based on their gamer type.

4.1.1.1 Tailoring Educational Technologies for Achiever Students

According to Orji's guideline, Achievers are a more individualistic type, preferring individual activities. They prefer to receive *(i)* Points, Badges, and Trophies as rewards for their performance in the activities, and *(ii)* they are better stimulated if they are surprised during their experience in the system. Based on Orji's guideline, in this study, the PT strategies, Cooperation, Rewards, Self-monitoring, and Suggestions, were used to tailor gamified educational systems to the Achiever's gamer types.

For this specific gamer type, the system must provide different missions to be solved individually, and these activities must provide Points, Badges, and Trophies, according to their results in the educational activities. This Personalization must occur because the Achiever gamer type is motivated by the PT strategies—Cooperation, Reward, Self-monitoring, and Suggestion. Cooperation uses game mechanics such as Communal Discovery and Social Fabric of Games, implementing activities to be solved in teams, together with colleagues. Reward uses game mechanics such as Physical Items, Virtual Items, Lottery, and Points, proposing the distribution of Virtual Items to reward players, giving players fee gifts and the opportunity of winning those. Self-monitoring and Suggestions use the game mechanics Quest, Achievement Levels, Loss Aversion, and Repeating Simple Actions, providing Points and allowing the players to follow their progress without punishing them.

The Reward PT strategy also addresses two other game mechanics (Reward Schedules and Bonuses) that use variable and fixed reward intervals to encourage performance and use the rewards to overcome challenges, reinforcing desired behavior. So, it is a good strategy to provide surprise rewards in variable and fixed intervals, to engage and motivate them. The process of tailoring gamified educational systems for the seven *BrainHex* gamer types developed and evaluated in this study considers the structure presented in Table 4.3.

In order to start the process, the students are required to create a profile, inserting their personal data (the initial data should be required according to each system, such as name, school, login, password, and others) after the student inserts the initial data. The gamer type is identified through the *BrainHex* questionnaire. In preexisting systems, the *BrainHex* questionnaire can attach to the system.

Next, the student can log into the system and perform the activities and solve the exercises (after the first student logs into the system, he will receive the default activities, then being able to access and perform the educational activities, without interference of the pedagogical model of the system). The gamification model of the system will be tailored based on the student's gamer type, so the user will receive the specific game design elements according to their gamer type (i.e., Points, Badges, Trophies, and Surprise Rewards, according to the Achiever's gamer type preferences).

The activities' flow and conduction do not receive any influence of the proposed structure. However, these activities generate Points, Badges, Trophies, and Surprise Rewards to the students, according to the student's performance in the system. The system also provides profile visualization, and this page provides options for the students to see their Points, Badges, Trophies, and Rewards in an organized manner on the scream. Table 4.4 and the Fig. 4.6 present a systematic sequence that should be followed to implement the tailored system for Achiever students.

4.1.1.2 Tailoring Educational Technologies for Conqueror Students

According to Orji's guideline, Conquerors are more interested in winning Medals or Badges to show and share their achievements, as well as comparing their results with

Table 4.4 Tailoring the design for the achiever gamer type

Gamer type	Persuasive strategies	Steps
Achiever	Cooperation, Reward, Self-monitoring and Suggestion	1. Registration in the system
		1.1. Personal data
		1.1.1. Gamer Type identification
		1.1.2. Login to the system
		1.1.3. Provide different educational activities to solve individually and/or collaboratively
		2. Provide Points, Badges, and Trophies, according to their result in each mission
		3. Provide surprise rewards for the conducted activities

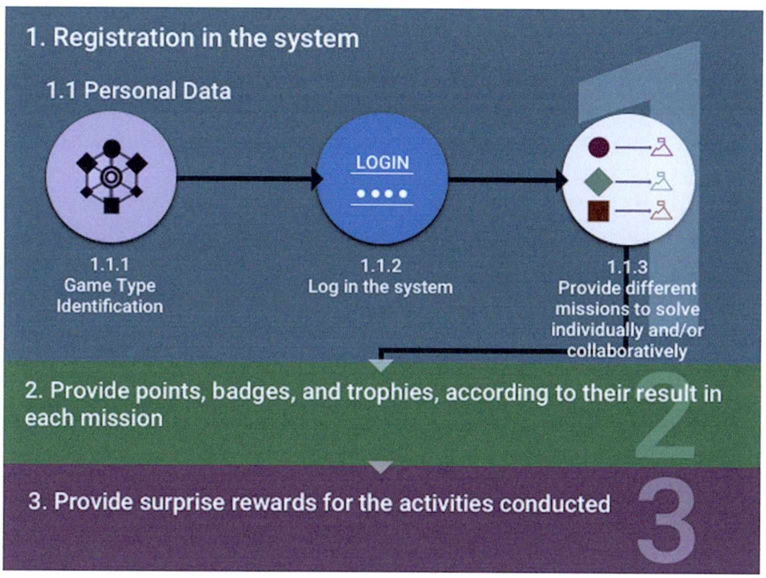

Fig. 4.6 Achiever approach

their colleagues. They prefer to receive: *(i)* Rankings with their achievements and position in Comparison with the other users, and *(ii)* they are better stimulated if they received activities with Limited time competing for Badges. Based on Orji's guideline in this study, the PT strategies, Competition and Comparison, Simulation and Personalization, were used to tailor gamified educational systems to the Conqueror gamer type.

With this gamer type, the system must provide different missions to be solved individually and with a time limit. These activities must provide Rankings according to the individual achievements. This Personalization must occur because the PT strategies used to motivate this gamer type (Competition and Comparison, simulation and Personalization) use mechanics such as Status and Leaderboards, in which the Ranking of the players to force them to compare and therefore compete.

The Competition and Comparison PT strategy also use the game mechanics Countdown and Leaderboard that provide a limited amount of time for the student to complete the challenges, and display high scores in Leaderboards, introducing Competition and Comparison. So, it is a good strategy to provide an individual Comparison of players and provide a Limited time for them to complete some activities. The approach of tailoring gamified educational system for Conquerors, proposed in this chapter, also uses the structure presented in Table 4.3.

After the Conqueror student logs into the system, they can access the available educational activities and perform them without the influence of the proposed structure, but with a time limit. These activities will award Badges to the students. The students can also access their profile and see their Badges and the Overall Ranking (generated by their Badges) with their position, and view a Comparison between them and their colleagues in a similar position.

Next, the Table 4.5 and the Fig. 4.7 present the specific approach to tailor gamified educational system for the Conquerors' gamer type. The approach is organized in three different steps, the first step being the general structure that must be provided by the system (Registration in the system, Personal data, Gamer Type identification, and Login into the system), and different kinds of educational activities and missions to be solved individually. The second step is to provide a Ranking with Leaderboard, Timeline, and Badges, according to the student's results in each mission in the system. Finally, the last step of the process is to provide a time limit for the students to conduct their educational activities and an Adapted Background History according to the student's gender.

Table 4.5 Tailoring design for the conqueror gamer type

Gamer type	Persuasive strategies	Steps
Conqueror	Competition and Comparison, Simulation, and Personalization	1. Registration in the system
		1.1. Personal data
		1.1.1. Gamer Type identification
		1.1.2. Login into the system
		1.1.3. Provide different educational activities to be solved individually
		2. Provide Ranking, Leaderboard, Timeline, and Badges, according to the student's results in each mission
		3. Provide limited time for the students to conduct their activities and adapted background history according to the student's gender

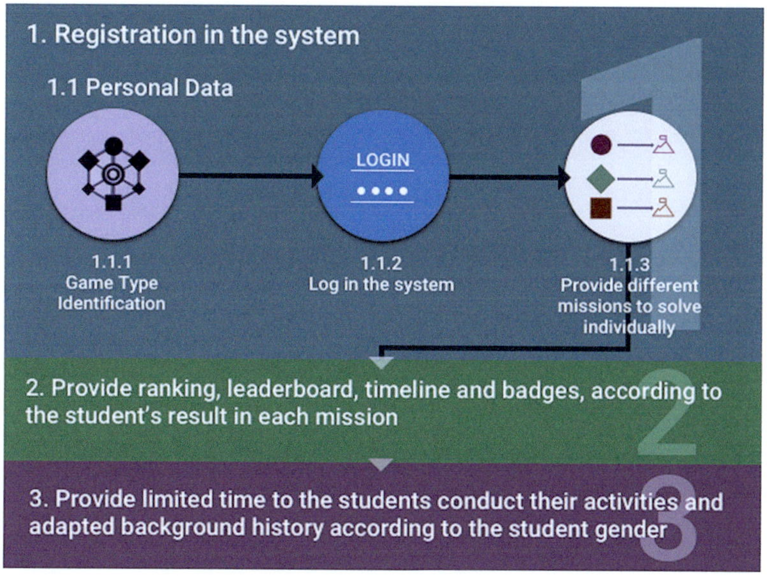

Fig. 4.7 Conqueror approach

4.1.1.3 Tailoring Educational Technologies for Daredevil Students

Based on Orji's guideline, Daredevils are more interested in showing and sharing their achievements with their colleagues, monitoring their performance gradually and according to their activities on the system. They prefer to: *(i)* receive Rankings with their achievements and positions in Comparison with the other users; *(ii)* be able to monitor the sequence of their activities and achievements. Based on the results of this study, the PT strategy Simulation was used to tailor gamified educational systems for the Daredevil gamer type, as defined by Orji et al. [2].

To this gamer type, the system must provide different missions to be solved individually. These activities must provide Rankings according to their individual achievements (Points can be used to calculate the Ranking, but the Points should not be displayed prominently, they should only be used to calculate the student's Rank). This Personalization must happen because the PT strategy used to motivate this gamer type (Simulation) uses game mechanics such as a Progress bar, and the Ranking must be used to force them to compare and therefore compete with one another.

After the Daredevil students log into the system, they can access the available educational activities inside and perform these activities, without any influence by the proposed structure. These activities can generate Points (used only to calculate the Ranking) and must be monitored by a Progress bar (the Progress bar also should be organized according to a group of activities). The student can also access their profile and see the Ranking (generated by their Points) with their position, and see

Table 4.6 Tailoring design for the Daredevil gamer type

Gamer type	Persuasive strategies	Steps
Daredevil	Simulation	1. Registration in the system
		1.1. Personal data
		1.1.1. Gamer Type identification
		1.1.2. Login into the system
		1.1.3. Provide different educational activities to be solved individually
		2. Provide Ranking, Leaderboard and a Progress bar, according to the student's result in each mission
		3. Provide background history according to student's gender

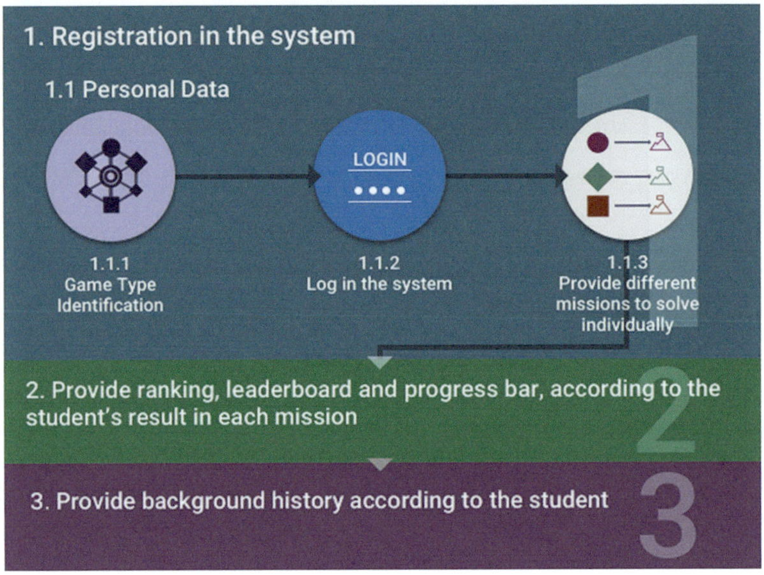

Fig. 4.8 Daredevil approach

a Comparison between themselves and their colleagues with a similar position. The profile should also provide a general Progress bar of their activities into the system.

Next, Table 4.6 and Fig. 4.8 present the specific process to tailor gamified educational systems to the Daredevils' gamer type. The process is organized into three different steps: the first being the general structure that must be provided by the system (Registration in the system, Personal data, Gamer Type identification, and Login into the system), and the different kind of educational activities to be solved individually; the second step is to provide a Ranking, Leaderboard and Progress bar, according to the student's results in each mission; finally, the last step of the process is to provide an adapted background history according to the student's gender.

4.1.1.4 Tailoring Educational Technologies for Mastermind Students

According to Orji's guideline, the Mastermind is a gamer type motivated by different game design elements. They have interest in showing and sharing their achievements with their colleagues and monitoring their performance gradually, according to their activities on the system and winning different prizes, such as Points and Badges. They prefer to receive: *(i)* an Adapted History on the system, *(ii)* Rankings with their achievements and position in Comparison with the other users, *(iii)* monitoring of their activities and achievements sequences, and *(iv)* Points and Badges for their activities. Based on Orji's guideline, in this study, the Self-monitoring–Suggestion and Competition–Comparison PT strategies were used to tailor gamified educational systems for the Mastermind gamer type.

For this gamer type, the system must provide different educational activities to be solved individually, related to an Adapted History during their activities on the system. These activities must also provide Points, Badges, and Rankings according to the individual achievements. This Personalization must occur because the PT strategies used to motivate this gamer type (Self-monitoring–Suggestion and Competition–Comparison–Personalization) use game mechanics such as Progress bar, Points, and Badges, using the player's Ranking to force them to compare and therefore compete with one another.

After the Mastermind student logs into the system, they can access the available educational activities and perform these activities, without any influence of the proposed structure. These activities can be provided with a time limit and generate Points and Badges. The student can follow his progress and performance through a Progress bar. The student can also access their profile and see the Ranking with their position, which presents a Comparison among their colleagues with a similar position. The profile also must provide a general Progress bar of their activities on the system.

In this overview of the system, the system provides the default educational activities for the students and an Adapted History to each student. The system also provides the option for the students to see their progress on the profile, as well as their Points, Badges, and Ranking, including their position with a Comparison between themselves and their colleagues with a similar position.

Next, Table 4.7 and Fig. 4.9 present the specific approach to tailor gamified educational system for the Mastermind gamer type. The process is organized into three different steps, with the first step being the general structure that must be provided by the system (Registration in the system, Personal data, Gamer Type identification, and Login into the system), and the different educational activities to be solved individually. The second step is to provide Points, Badges, Progress bar, and Ranking (with Leaderboards) according to the students' results in each mission. Finally, the

Table 4.7 Tailoring design for the Mastermind gamer type

Gamer type	Persuasive strategies	Steps
Mastermind	Self-monitoring and Suggestion, Competition, Comparison, and Personalization	1. Registration in the system
		1.1. Personal data
		1.1.1. Gamer Type identification
		1.1.2. Login into the system
		1.1.3. Provide different educational activities to solve individually
		2. Provide Points, Badges, Progress bar, Ranking, and Leaderboards according to the student's results in each mission
		3. Provide a time limit and adapted background history according to the student's gender

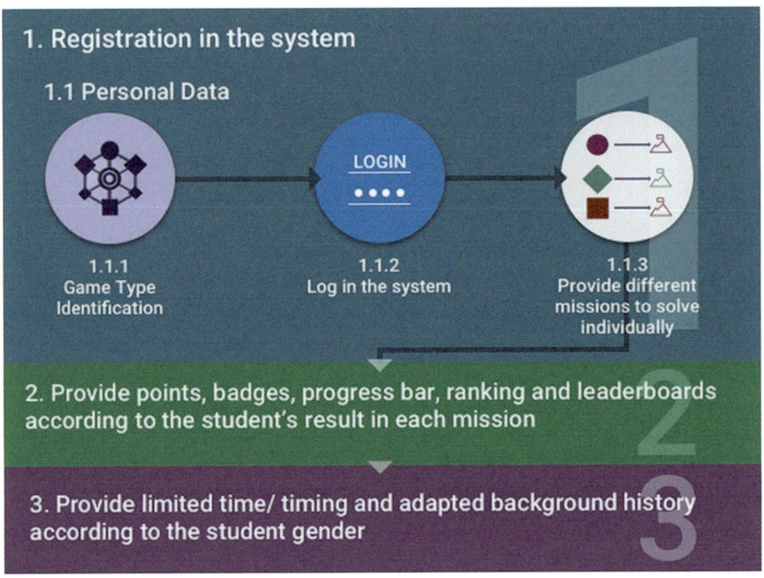

Fig. 4.9 Mastermind approach

last step of the process is to provide a time limit and an Adapted Background History according to the student's gender.

4.1.1.5 Tailoring Educational Technologies for Seeker Students

The Seekers, according to Orji's guideline, are more motivated by the opportunity to choose their prizes, such as receiving different options of Badges or Trophies. This gamer type is motivated when comparing their prizes with their colleagues. They are also interested in following an Adapted History. They prefer to receive: *(i)* an Adapted History on the system; *(ii)* Rankings with their achievements and position in Comparison with the other users, and *(iii)* prizes that can be chosen during the game or when they are using the system. Based on Orji's guideline, the PT strategies, Customization–Personalization and Competition–Comparison, were used to tailor gamified educational system to Seekers gamer types.

For this gamer type, the system must provide different educational activities to be solved individually, related to an Adapted History during their activities on the system. These activities must provide a different set of prizes (i.e., Badges and Trophies), according to their individual achievements and preferences, and a Ranking with Leaderboards. This Personalization must occur because the PT strategies used to motivate this gamer type (Customization-Personalization and Competition–Comparison) use game mechanics such as Adapted History, Ranking, and different prizes to be chosen by the student. The approach of tailoring gamified educational systems for Seekers that was developed and evaluated inside this work also considers the structure presented in Table 4.3.

After the Seeker student logs into the system, they can access the educational activities available and perform these activities, without any influence of the proposed structure. These activities can generate Points (only used to calculate the Ranking). They also should receive an Adapted History, be able to access their profile to see the Ranking with their position and see a Comparison between them and their colleagues with a similar position. Next, Table 4.8 and Fig. 4.10 present the specific approach to tailor gamified educational systems to the Seeker gamer type.

The process is organized into four different steps: the first step being the general structure that should be provided by the system (Registration in the system, Personal data, Gamer Type identification, and Login into the system), and the different educational activities to be solved individually; the second step is to provide a Ranking (with Leaderboards) according to the student's result in each activity; in the third step, the system must provide the opportunity for the students to choose their prizes; finally, the last step of the process is to provide a time limit and an Adapted History according to the student's gender.

Table 4.8 Tailoring design for the seeker gamer type

Gamer type	Persuasive strategies	Steps
Seeker	Customization, Personalization and Competition and Comparison	1. Registration in the system
		1.1. Personal data
		1.1.1. Gamer Type identification
		1.1.2. Login into the system
		1.1.3. Provide different educational activities to solve individually
		2. Provide a Ranking and Leaderboards according to the students' results in each mission
		3. Provide the opportunity for the students to choose their prizes
		4. Provide a time limit and an adapted background history according to the student's gender

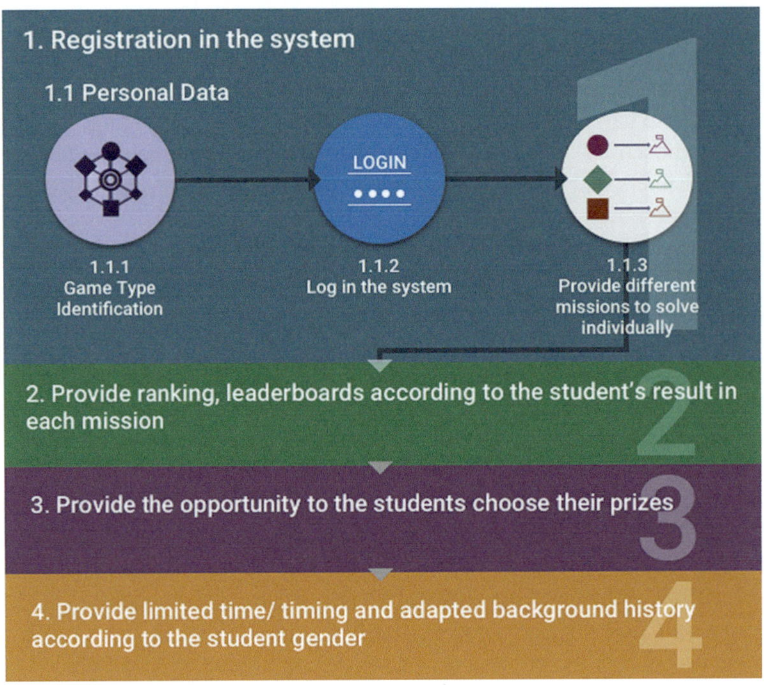

Fig. 4.10 Seeker approach

4.1.1.6 Tailoring Educational Technologies for Socializer Students

According to Orji's guideline, Socializers are more interested in showing their performance to other people and sharing their achievements, as well as comparing their results with other colleagues. They usually: *(i)* prefer to receive Rankings with their Points and positions in Comparison with the other users; and *(ii)* are better stimulated if they receive a direct Comparison with their colleagues that have a similar number of Points and positions. Based on Orji's guideline, the PT strategy Competition and Comparison were used in our proposal to tailor gamified educational systems for Socializers.

For this specific gamer type, the system must provide different educational activities to be solved individually, and these activities must provide Rankings according to the individual study Points. This Personalization must occur because the Socializer gamer type is motivated by the PT strategies Cooperation–Competition–Comparison. Competition and Comparison use the game mechanics Status and the player's Ranking to force them to compare and therefore compete with each other, and when the student see the other players' achievements, they will strive to reach their status, therefore increasing Competition and Comparison.

The PT strategy Competition and Comparison also use the game mechanics Countdown and Leaderboard that provide a time limit for the student to complete their challenges. Also, displaying high scores in the Leaderboards will increase Competition and Comparison. So, it is a good strategy to provide an individual Comparison of players with a similar number of Points, such as using a specific type of Ranking, and providing a time limit for the students to complete some activities. The approach of tailoring gamified educational systems for the Socializer gamer type developed in this chapter considers the structure presented in Table 4.10 and Fig. 4.11.

The Socializer student logs into the system and accesses its available activities to execute them. These activities do not receive any influence of the proposed structure. They will generate Points for the student based on their performance in the activities.

Table 4.9 Tailoring design for the Socializer gamer type

Gamer type	Persuasive strategy	Steps
Socializer	Cooperation, Competition and Comparison	1. Registration in the system
		1.2. Personal data
		1.1.1. Gamer Type identification
		1.1.2. Login into the system
		1.1.3. Provide different educational activities to be solved individually and/or collaboratively
		2. Provide Rankings and Leaderboards according to the individual Points
		3. Provide a time limit for the students to conduct their activities

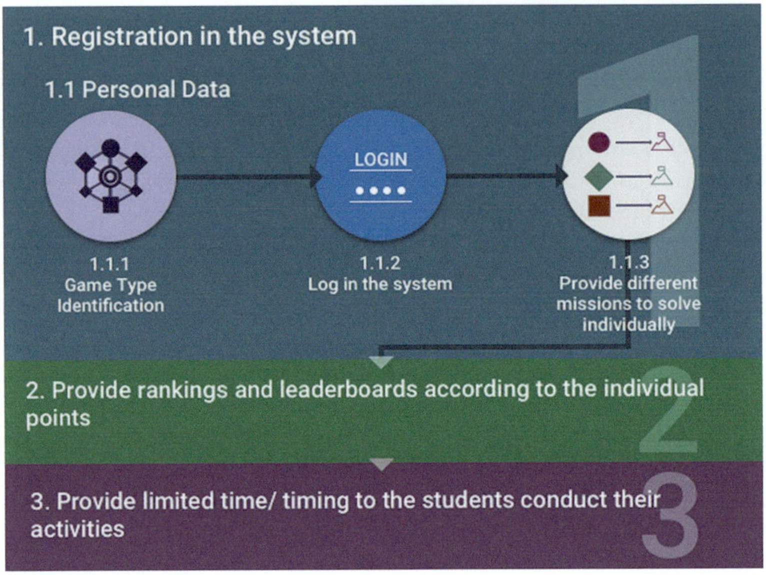

Fig. 4.11 Socializer approach

The student can also access their profile and view the Ranking (based on their Points) with their position, and see a Comparison between their colleagues with a similar position.

The approach is organized into three different steps, with the first being the general structure that must be provided by the system (Registration in the system, Personal data, Gamer Type identification, and Login into the system), and the type of activities provided, with the different missions to be solved individually and/or collaboratively. The second step is to provide a Ranking and Leaderboards according to the student's result in each mission. In the third step, the system should provide the opportunity for the students to choose their prizes. Finally, the last step of the process is to provide a time limit for the students to conduct their activities (Table 4.9).

4.1.1.7 Tailoring Educational Technologies for Survivor Students

Survivors are more interested in following and showing their performance to other people, sharing and comparing their achievements and results with their colleagues. They usually: *(i)* prefer to receive Points and a Progress bar to follow their progress; *(ii)* are better stimulated if they receive a Ranking with Leaderboards to compare their performance with their colleagues; and *(iii)* are also motivated if the system provides a time limit to conduct the activities/tasks. Based on Orji's guideline, the PT strategies Self-monitoring–Suggestion and Competition–Comparison were used to tailor gamified educational systems for the survivor gamer type.

For this specific gamer type, the system must provide different missions to be solved individually, with these activities providing Rankings according to the individual study Points. This Personalization occurs because the Survivors are more motivated by the PT strategies Self-monitoring–Suggestion and Competition–Comparison, using the game mechanics Status and the player's Ranking to force them to compare and therefore compete.

The PT strategy Competition and Comparison also use the game mechanics Countdown and Leaderboard that provide a limited amount of time for the student to complete the challenge, and displaying high scores in Leaderboards will increase Competition and Comparison. Therefore, it is a good strategy to provide an individual Comparison of players with a similar number of Points, such as using a specific type of Ranking and providing a time limit for the students to complete some activities. The approach of tailoring gamified educational systems for Survivors proposed considers the structure presented in Table 4.3.

The Survivor student logs into the system and access its available educational activities to execute them. These activities do not receive any influence of the proposed structure. They will generate Points for the student based on their performance in the activities (with a time limit). The student can also access their profile and view the Ranking with Leaderboards showing their position, as well as his Points and a Progress bar.

Next, Table 4.10 and Fig. 4.12 present the specific approach to tailor gamified educational systems for the Survivor gamer type. The process is organized into three different steps, with the first being the general structure that should be provided by the system (Registration in the system, Personal data, Gamer Type identification, and Login into the system), and the type of different missions to be solved individually and/or collaboratively. The second step is to provide Points, Progress bar, and Ranking (with Leaderboards), according to the student's results in each mission. Finally, the last step of the process is to provide a Time Limit for the students to conduct their activities.

Table 4.10 Tailoring design for the survivor gamer type

Gamer type	Persuasive strategies	Steps
Survivor	Self-monitoring–Suggestion and Competition–Comparison	1. Registration in the system
		1.1. Personal data
		1.1.1. Gamer Type identification
		1.1.2. Login into the system
		1.1.3. Provide different educational activities to be solved individually
		2. Provide Points, Progress bar, Ranking, and Leaderboards according to the student's results in each mission
		3. Provide a time limit for the students to conduct their activities

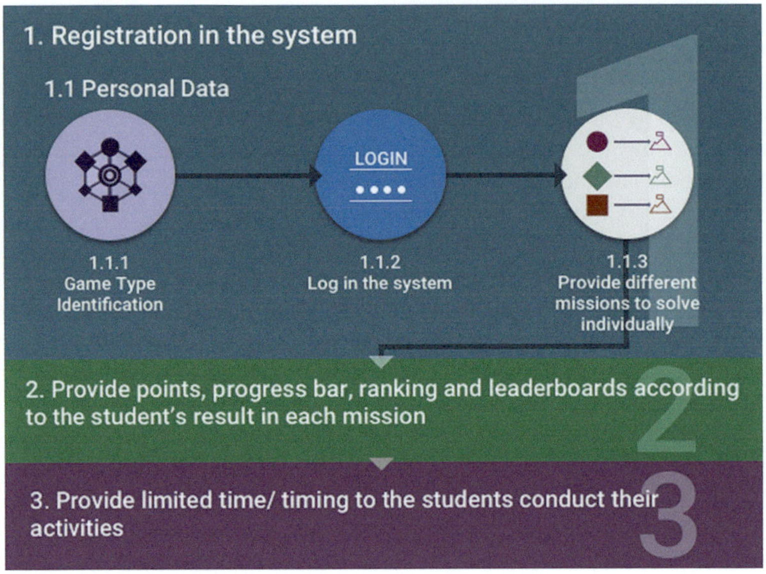

Fig. 4.12 Survivor approach

References

1. R. Orji, R.L. Mandryk, J. Vassileva, K.M. Gerling, Tailoring persuasive health games to gamer type, in *Proceedings of the SIGCHI Conference on Human Factors in Computing Systems* (ACM, 2013), pp. 2467–2476
2. R. Orji, R.L. Mandryk, J. Vassileva, Selecting effective strategies for tailoring persuasive health games to gamer types (2014)
3. J. Hamari, J. Koivisto, H. Sarsa. Does gamification work?–a literature review of empirical studies on gamification, in *2014 47th Hawaii International Conference on System Sciences (HICSS)* (IEEE, 2014), pp. 3025–3034
4. F.F.-H. Nah, Q. Zeng, V.R. Telaprolu, A.P. Ayyappa, B. Eschenbrenner, Gamification of education: a review of literature, in *International conference on hci in business* (Springer, 2014), pp. 401–409
5. P. Schuytema. *Game Design: A Practical Approach*. Number Sirsi) i9781584504719 (Charles River Media, Needham, 2007)
6. D. Dicheva, C. Dichev, Gamification in education: where are we in 2015? in *E-Learn: World Conference on E-Learning in Corporate, Government, Healthcare, and Higher Education*. Association for the Advancement of Computing in Education (AACE) (2015), pp. 1445–1454
7. T. Fullerton, *Game Design Workshop: A Playcentric Approach to Creating Innovative Games* (CRC Press, Boca Raton, 2014)

Chapter 5
Selecting the Most Suitable Gamification Elements for Each Situation

Abstract Recent studies have shown that using gamification may negatively impact the motivation of students in educational systems. One of the reasons for this problem is that people may be motivated or demotivated by different gamification elements according to their gamer type, gender, age, and other particularities. In this chapter, we aim to investigate whether student's gamer types and gender have different perceptions in terms of gamification elements preferences. We will present a result from an empirical experiment conducted with 121 Brazilian elementary students, applying a survey to identify their preferences about the ten most popular gamification elements used along with educational systems. Our results suggest that there are no significant differences in terms of student's gamer types and gender preferences for most of the gamification elements. However, we identified that they prefer particular elements against others. As such, these results confirm the importance of conducting new studies in tailored gamification for educational systems.

5.1 Gamification Mechanics and Gamification Elements

Throughout history, many have advocated the use of play, games, and game-inspired design to improve the human condition [1]. Recently, gamification has become a popular method for enriching information technologies, and it has been used in different types of systems, including the educational ones [2]. The term "gamification," according to [3], was first used in 2008, in a blog post by Brett Terrill, describing the word as "taking game mechanics and applying them to other web properties to increase engagement." However, the concept of gamification has been commonly adopted by the digital media industry [4]. The first documented use dates back to 2008 by Paharia [5], but the term has not been widely adopted before the second half of 2010 [4].

During the last couple of years, gamification has been a trending topic and a subject of much hype as a means of supporting user engagement and enhancing positive patterns in service use [2]. Gamification has been researched and discussed in several different contexts, for instance, in the general academic context (e.g., Sinha [6] and Challco et al. [7]), industry (e.g., Korolov et al. [8] and Herger et al. [9])

W. Oliveira and I. I. Bittencourt, *Tailored Gamification to Educational Technologies*,
https://doi.org/10.1007/978-981-32-9812-5_5

among others. Some have conducted empirical experiments in order to identify the real effects of applying gamification on people behavior, learning, and so on (e.g., Hamari et al. [10] and Santana et al. [11]). More specifically, in the academia context (main interest of this study), these works have been done, especially in gamification applied to C&E, in order to provide student's motivation and engagement in learning environments.

According to Hamari et al. [2] and Nacke et al. [1], the first wave of gamification research has often composed of definitions, frameworks, and taxonomies about gamification and game design elements; technical studies presenting gamified systems, architectures and designs; and the effect gamified systems in the users. These trends of studies have pointed out many challenges in this field.

Nowadays, different definitions of gamification have been used in the academia; Deterding et al. [4] define the concept of gamification, as "the use of game design elements in non-game contexts." Werbach [12], in turn, uses a designer's point of view and address a general definition of gamification as "the process of making activities more game-like," aiming to bring academics and practitioners prospect approximately together.

Huotari and Hamari [13] define the concept of gamification as a service framework where the main service is appreciated by a group of rules system providing interaction mechanisms and feedback to the users in order to aid and support the overall value creation for the users. More recently, Huotari and Hamari [14] updated this term proposing a definition for gamification, anchoring gamification in the service marketing literature, as follows: "gamification refers to a process of enhancing a service with affordances for gameful experiences in order to support users overall value creation."

In order to synthesize the terms, Pedro [15] addresses gamification as a term directly related to the concept of games and game mechanics. Gamification has grouped a plethora of rules, patterns, and feedbacks to provide user's engagement and motivation and can be applied to develop game-like mechanics in different applications, including educational systems [15]. Pedro and Vassileva [15] describes the most used game-like mechanics in gamified systems. We show these game mechanics in Table 5.1, summarized by Pedro et al. [15].

Table 5.1 Patterns of game mechanics (summarized by Pedro et al. [15])

Pattern	Description
Ownership	Allowing the user to own things, such as Points, token, Badges. It creates loyalty to the system
Achievements	Providing a virtual or physical representation of having accomplished something that can be easy, difficult, surprising, funny, and accomplished alone or as a group
Status	Computing and displaying rank or level or a user
Community collaboration and quests	Posing challenges to the users related to time limit or competition that can be resolved by working together

Gamification takes power from games and applies it to a given context in order to solve a problem. An important aspect of gamification is the understanding of which game elements are adequate for each problem and situation. Werbach and Hunter [12] describe game elements as "smaller pieces used to define building blocks that form the integrated gameplay experience." According to the same authors, these game elements are included in the dynamics, mechanics, and components categories [16], as described below:

- **Game dynamics**—the "big picture" aspects of the gamified system that need to be considered and managed and can never be direct into the game (e.g., constraints, emotions, narrative, progression, relationships, and personalization) [16].
- **Game mechanics**—the basic processes that drive the action forward and generate player engagement (e.g., challenges, change, competition, cooperation, feedback, resource, acquisition, rewards, transactions, turns, win states, and profiles) [16].
- **Game components**—also named game design elements, they are the specific instances of mechanics and dynamics (e.g., achievements, Badges, collections, leader boards, levels, notifications, Points, Progress bars, quests or missions, status, teams, virtual goods, and so on) [16].

While no standard conceptualization of gamification exists, most sources agree that gamification is generally defined as "the use of game elements and mechanics in non-game contexts" and a series of studies have been done in order to research the influence of gamification in the learning of students, especially in computer-based activities. In order to identify studies in gamification, Hamari et al. [2] conducted a systematic literature review (SLR), which aims to identify empirical studies in gamification, as well as to answer the question: Does gamification work?

Among the results, especially two are nowadays in this work: (*i*) most works about gamification with empirical results, have been from C&E [2], and (ii) all of the studies in education/learning contexts with learning outcomes of gamification considered mostly positive, for example, in terms of increased motivation and engagement in the learning tasks, as well as enjoyment over them. However, at the same time, the studies pointed out negative outcomes which need to be paid attention to, such as the effects of increased competition, task evaluation difficulties, and design features [2].

These results are most important to this study. First, to show the crescent amount of studies carried out in gamification applied to C&E, as well as to show the important positive results of its application in the motivation, engagement, and learning of students. Second, these results also show negative outcomes which need to be paid attention to, revealing that other studies in gamification are needed, especially in gamification applied to C&E.

In the face of this scenario, different recent studies have been pointing the design of gamification elements in education and conducting some studies in this domain. Nah et al. [17] conducted a literature review and presented the eight-game design elements that are used extensively in educational and learning contexts: (1) Points; (2) Levels/Stages; (3) Badges; (4) Leaderboards; (5) Prizes and Rewards; (6) Progress bars; (7) Storyline; and (8) Feedback.

In addition, Dicheva et al. [18] also identify the most used gamification elements in the field of education from a secondary study. In this study, Dicheva and her colleagues conducted a systematic mapping (SM) and identified the six most used gamification elements in the literature about gamification in education, which are: (1) Points; (2) Badges; (3) Levels; (4) Leaderboards; (5) Virtual goods; and (6) Avatars. Based on these findings and the literature on gamification elements, we summarized the results and collected the ten most popular gamification elements used in the field of education in Table 5.2:

Table 5.2 Gamification elements used in education (based on the Nah et al. [17] study)

Game element	Description
Points	The idea of "Points" is to measure the success or achievement of a player. This element can also be used as a reward, as a form of money or to calculate the progress of a user, as well as, to indicate a stage of user. Also exists the experience points (XP) (i.e., the earned points from a complete a tasks) and steam points (i.e., points to represent to in-game currency) used for some of the role-playing games in education O'Donovan et al. [19]. Points can also be considered like credits in some educational system Kumar and Khurana [20]
Levels/Stages	The "Level" element can be used in various kind of game to give players a feeling of progression in the system. Initial, levels tend to require a few efforts and are quicker to be earned. Even though levels (also named stages) are a widespread and popular concept used as a form to reward the users for task completion. The students' learning abilities may not progress or improve as a result of leveling Goehle [21]
Badges	The idea of "Badges" are represented a mark of appreciation or a step accomplishment during the process of goal achievement. In order to maintain students' motivation, the use of this element is interesting for engaging the learners in subsequent tasks. Badges are effective in inspiring learners to work toward future goals O'Donovan et al. [19]. The majority of the student respondents in Santos [22] survey also felt that Badges helped to keep them engaged, especially in the classroom context, and motivate them to carry out future learning tasks
Leaderboards	The objective of a "Leaderboard" is to keep the users engaged, creating a feeling of eagerness to advance their names for the achievements they have accomplished and compared their performance with that of other colleagues. A Leaderboard is also used to display the current levels of high scorers and the overall scores (usually the 5 to 10 names with the closest score are displayed). In the study conducted by O'Donovan et al. [19], they identified that Leaderboards rank highest in motivating learners

(continued)

Table 5.2 (continued)

Game element	Description
Prizes and Rewards	The use of "Prizes" has been found to be effective in motivating learners Brewer et al. [23]. The timing and scale of rewards can also affect learner motivation Raymer [24]. In general, it is better to give multiple small rewards than one big reward. Also, the schedule for giving out rewards should be evenly distributed throughout the learning process. An example of in-game rewards is character upgrades Raymer [24]. A character upgrade is a way to motivate learners by displaying their progress in the form of characters. It allows others to recognize the amount of effort a learner has spent to reach his or her current level. In order to use character upgrades as a game design element, one must be given a virtual character which allows him or her to upgrade from time-to-time by means of Points or rewards earned Raymer [24]
Progress bars	Several researchers (e.g., Berkling and Thomas [25], O'Donovan et al. [19], and Raymer [24] have utilized Progress bars to gamify education. While Badges demonstrate achievements toward a particular level/goal, Progress bars are used to display the general progression toward a goal. In an educational game, for instance, this element can be used to motivate the students who are close to achieving their aim in game or also to motivate them if they are falling to finish with their progress
Storyline	"Storyline" (also named narrative) is used to can help learners to achieve an ideal interest curve, through this element, the idea is to make a user of the system delve into a story that makes you feel like doing the proposed activities in a system in order to unravel the story behind. A storyline also can provide a background for learning and problem solving and help to illustrate applicability of concepts to real-life O'Donovan et al. [19]
Feedback	The frequency, intensity, and immediacy of feedback are helpful for learner's engagement (i.e., Berkling and Thomas [25], Kapp [26] and Raymer [24]). The more frequent and immediate the feedback is, the greater the learning effectiveness and learner engagement. Clear and immediate feedback has been shown to be important for attaining the flow state, which is a state of engagement and immersion in an activity (i.e., Nah et al. [17], Csikszentmihalyi [27] and Csikszentmihalyi [28]). Hence, feedback is an important criterion for performance and engagement

5.2 Selecting the Most Suitable Gamification Elements

In order to identify the most suitable gamification elements for each situation (considering student's gamer type and gender), we conducted an experimental study with 121 elementary school students enrolled in Brazilian private school. In this chapter, our focus will be on the results of the experiments. In order to obtain our results, we followed an experimental design. An experiment is a procedure carried out to support, refute, or validate a hypothesis, it provides insight into cause-and-effect by demonstrating what outcome occurs when a particular factor is manipulated [9, 29, 30].

This experiment aims to identify whether gamer types have different preferences in terms of gamification elements and then identify the most suitable gamification elements adapted to each gamer type. The participants were elementary school students. The experiment is classified as a "comparative experiment" with one factor (independent variable), which has ten possible values or "levels" (based on [9] and [31]), as further explained. This experiment was approved by the University of Saskatchewan Behavioral Research Ethics Board (Project BEH#16-142). In order to conduct our experiment, we used the Goal/Question/Metric (GQM) method. The GQM assumes that for an organization to measure in an accurate way it must:

1. Specify the goals for itself and its projects.
2. Trace those goals to the data that is intended to define those goals operationally.
3. Provide a framework to interpret the data regarding the goals that were established.

The main goal of the experiment is to evaluate students' preferences regarding the gamification elements, according to their gamer type, in gamified educational systems. The specific goals are presented as follows:

- To identify if the students' gamer types have different preferences about gamification elements in GES.
- To identify the most suitable gamification elements for each students' gamer type in GES.

Following the GQM method, according to the previously presented objectives, we defined our research questions:

RQ1. Do the students have different preferences about gamification elements according to their gamer type?

RQ2. What are the most suitable gamification elements to motivate each *BrainHex* student gamer type?

$H_{1\cdot 0\cdot 0}$: The Achiever students' preferences are similar for the gamification elements.

$H_{1\cdot 0\cdot 1}$: The Achiever students' preferences are different for the gamification elements.

$H_{2\cdot 1\cdot 0}$: The Conqueror students' preferences are similar for the gamification elements.

$H_{2\cdot 1\cdot 1}$: The Conqueror students' preferences are different for the gamification elements.

$H_{3\cdot 1\cdot 0}$: The Daredevil students' preferences are similar for the gamification elements.

$H_{3\cdot 1\cdot 1}$: The Daredevil students' preferences are different for the gamification elements.

$H_{4\cdot 1\cdot 0}$: The Mastermind students' preferences are similar for the gamification elements.

$H_{4\cdot 1\cdot 1}$: The Mastermind students' preferences are different for the gamification elements.

$H_{5\cdot 1\cdot 0}$: The Seeker students' preferences are similar for the gamification elements.

$H_{5 \cdot 1 \cdot 1}$: The Seeker students' preferences are different for the gamification elements.

$H_{6 \cdot 1 \cdot 0}$: The Socializer students' preferences are similar for the gamification elements.

$H_{6 \cdot 1 \cdot 1}$: The Socializer students' preferences are different for the gamification elements.

$H_{7 \cdot 1 \cdot 0}$: The Survivor students' preferences are similar for the gamification elements.

$H_{7 \cdot 1 \cdot 1}$: The Survivor students' preferences are different for the gamification elements.

$H_{8 \cdot 1 \cdot 0}$: The gender students' preferences are similar for the gamification elements.

$H_{8 \cdot 1 \cdot 1}$: The gender students' preferences are different for the gamification elements.

Based on the hypothesis defined above, our experiment has one factor, i.e., the gamification element (with ten different types of gamification elements). The response variables are the students' preferences. We defined a metric to measure these preferences in partnership with two specialists whose field of expertise is Statistical and Behavioral Science. The metric that was used was a 7-point Likert scale [32] from 1 to 7, where 1 meant "I hate this gamification element" and 7 "I love this gamification element." Our experimental unities are our sample composed of elementary students in interaction with gamification elements embedded in a survey.

We collected data from 121 Brazilian elementary school students, among whom 52 were males and 69 were females, aged between 11 and 13 years old (average age of 12 years old). This age range was chosen especially due to the lack of studies investigating the influence of the gamification elements on elementary school students. Table 5.3 organizes our sample according to the student's gamer types.

To identify the student's gamer type, the *BrainHex* questionnaire was applied in the beginning of our survey. In order to identify students' preferences regarding gamification elements, a survey containing ten questions was applied. In the survey, gamification elements were presented to the students as a storytelling, following the recommendations of [33], to create illustrative storytelling with a simple expla-

Table 5.3 Sample of experiment

Gamer type	Sample	Male	Female
Achiever	48	18	30
Conqueror	28	15	12
Daredevil	6	5	1
Mastermind	3	0	3
Seeker	16	5	11
Socializer	9	5	4
Survivor	12	4	8
Total	121	52	69

nation about the gamification element (explaining what that gamification element represents, how it behaves in the system and what are its consequences) and an illustrative example of each gamification element. After viewing each gamification element, the students were asked to answer about their level of preference for each element (in the 7-point Likert scale). In order to collect the students' gender information, one of the questions on the survey asked the students about their gender, with three options: "Male," "Female," and "I prefer not to answer." Responses marked as "I prefer not to answer" would not be considered in our study, although we did not receive any answer choosing this option. Following recent studies in this field [34–36], and in order to simplify the process, we only considered the data for two genders (female and male). The number of participants who were self-identified as other genders is, in general, too small to allow us to conduct statistical analysis.

We used the one-way analysis of variation (ANOVA) and the Tukey's test. ANOVA is a technique that can be used to compare means of two or more samples (using the F distribution). This technique can be used only for numerical answers data, which is named "Y" and is usually one variable, and numerical or categorical input data, named "X," which is always one variable, hence the "one-way" [37]. Tukey's test is a single-step, multiple comparison procedure, and statistical test. It can be used on raw data or in conjunction with an ANOVA (post hoc analysis) to find means that are significantly different from each other [38]. Tukey's test compares the means of every treatment, applying simultaneously to the sets of all pairwise comparisons and identifying any difference between two means that is greater than the expected standard error. To compare whether male and female users have different preferences regarding specific elements, e.g., if males prefer the gamification element Badge more than females, we used the t-test [39].

5.2.1 A Guideline to Tailor Gamified Educational System with the Most Suitable Gamification Elements Based on Student's Gamer Type and Gender

We conducted in this experiment a comparative analysis addressing gamification elements preferences, to identify the preferences of *BrainHex* gamer types in terms of gamification elements. The study was conducted with Brazilian elementary school students and our general findings indicate some similarities with recent studies in this field. However, it added new findings for the literature. In summary, we intended to answer two different research questions: *(i)* Do the students have different preferences about the gamification elements according to their gamer type? And, *(ii)* what are the most suitable gamification elements to motivate each student gamer type?

Regarding the first research question, our findings indicated that there is a statistical difference in terms of gamification elements in some of the gamer types analyzed. Some other gamer types (e.g., Seeker) did not present a really significative difference in terms of gamification elements preferences. The results confirmed the outcome of some recent studies in this field, emphasizing that this gamer type is motivated by the opportunity of choosing his prizes [8].

Regarding the gamification elements, our study confirmed that most of the gamer types have different individual preferences. In the case of the Achiever students, our results recommend the use of five different gamification elements: Points, Progress bar, Trophies, Avatars, and Badges. These elements belong to the group of elements used to stimulate players to compete, win challenges and collect their achievements. Other elements, such as History, Ranking, and Levels, can be used in the system. However, they will not motivate the students. On the other hand, if the system uses the elements Feedback and Timeline, it can be harmful to the students with this player type.

About the Conquerors, our findings indicate that the systems can use six different gamification elements to motivate these students: Points, Badges, Levels, Progress bar, Ranking, and Avatars. These elements are used specially to motivate the students to compete and follow their progress in the system. The elements Trophies and History also can be used. However, based on our results, maybe they could not be well accepted by the students. Like with the Achievers, the use of Feedback and Timeline must be avoided in the system.

To tailor the systems for the Daredevil students, according to our results, five different elements should be used: Levels, Trophies, Avatars, Badges, and Ranking. These elements also represent a way to motivate students to compete and follow their progress in the system. Points and Feedback can also be used; however, they could not bring benefits to the students. Three gamification elements (Timeline, History, and Progress bar) should be avoided to tailor gamified educational systems for this gamer type. At the same time, our results can also confirm a recent study [8], as it also showed that the Seekers seem to like all the elements, being motivated by the opportunity of choosing their prizes.

Our results indicate that the Socializers are motivated by the gamification elements Points, Ranking, Avatars, Badges, and Levels, elements especially used to help students create an identity within the system, increasing their level in it. The elements Feedback, Progress bar, and History can also be used to help the students to create a social identity within the system. On the other hand, the elements Timeline and Trophies should be avoided in systems tailored to the Socializer students.

In our study, the findings indicate that, for the Survivor students, the gamification elements Avatars, Badges, and Ranking should be used to motivate them. The elements Levels, Progress bar, History, and Trophies, can also be used; however, they may be significant for the Survivors motivation. The elements Points and Timeline should be avoided in tailored systems for the survivors.

To provide a better solution to implement tailored gamified educational systems based on student's gamer types and student's gender, we will provide in this section a guideline for the gamification designers and programmers to implement the systems. The guidelines will be organized into two different categories: (*i*) guideline to tailor new systems and (*ii*) guidelines to modify pre-existent systems.

One of the main challenges is to create new gamified educational systems adapted according to the students' gamer types. To implement this type of system, we created a guideline based on the results. The guideline is composed by five main steps: (*i*) selecting a gamification framework; (*ii*) designing the system architecture; (*iii*) implementing the tailored model; (*iv*) identifying the students' gamer types; and (*v*) providing the adapted interface. We also recommend evaluating the students' satisfaction with the system after they use it.

In the first step, we recommend beginning the project by selecting a gamification framework to design the general gamification model of the system. This gamification framework will help the gamification designers to implement the general gamification design, according to the goals of the system. Many different gamification frameworks are available to be used to implement the gamified systems (to a comprehensive review about gamification design frameworks, see Mora et al. [40]).

In the second step, we recommend designing the architectural base of the system. In this step, it is important to associate the general system architectural base with an architectural design approach to provide the different versions of the system. This step consists of associating the general system architectural design and process with our proposed architectural design and process.

In the third step, we recommend the implementation of the tailored model. This model should be developed based on our process, to select the best gamification elements for each gamer type. In this step, it is important to provide the ten most used educational gamification elements [17, 18], associating these gamification elements to each *BrainHex* gamer type.

Finally, we recommend identifying the students' gamer types using the *BrainHex* player model (or equivalent) and providing the adapted system interface based on the students' gamer types. In this step, it is important to consider the *BrainHex* player type to identify the students' gamer types. However, recent studies have provided theoretical correlations between the different player types (e.g., Hamari and Tuunanen [41]). Figure 5.1 presents the diagram to implement new adapted gamified educational systems.

Another great challenge is to adapt existing systems; this is a big challenge because these systems were not originally designed to provide an adapted gamification model to the students. In this sense, it can be hard to tailor these systems. However, we want to provide a guideline to adapt the gamification design of existent gamified educational systems based on the students' gamer types. We recommend conducting this process in four main steps: (*i*) identifying the students' gamer types; (*ii*) associating our architectural design with the original system architectural design; (*iii*) implementing the tailored model; and (*iv*) providing the adapted interface (in terms of gamification elements).

In the first step, we recommend using the *BrainHex* player model (or equivalent) to identify the students' gamer type. It is important to highlight that in existing systems, it may be necessary to provide some mechanism so that students can respond to the *BrainHex* questionnaire.

In the second step, we recommend associating our architectural design with the original system architectural design. To provide the different versions of the system, we recommend implementing the tailored model, based on our process. In this step, it is important to identify what will be needed to design new gamification elements.

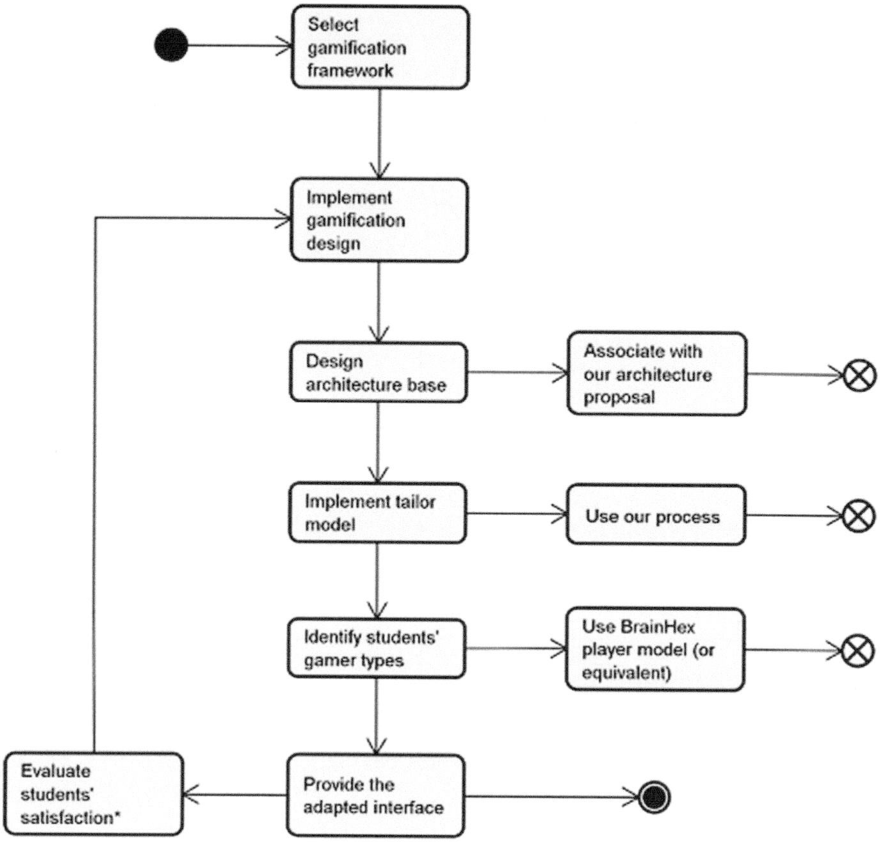

Fig. 5.1 Guideline to tailor new TGES based on gamer types

For instance, in the original system, some gamification elements (i.e., Ranking or Points) that are significant for some specific gamer types may not have been created. In this case, it is important to create these gamification elements, to provide a better personalization.

Finally, we recommend providing an adapted interface for each gamer type. The adapted interface can be changed slowly to avoid abrupt changes in the system interface (new studies need to be carried out in order to identify the consequences of abrupt changes in gamified interfaces). Figure 5.2 presents the diagram for the adapted GES. In order to finish this chapter, Table 5.4 presents the most suitable gamification elements for each gamer type identified in our study, Table 5.5 presents the neutral gamification elements for each gamer type, and Table 5.6 presents the possible worst gamification elements for each gamer type.

Considering the design of a system with five gamification elements (in general a more robust system, for a large number of activities and students), the gamification elements may be similar for both genders, as highlighted in Fig. 5.3. The gamification

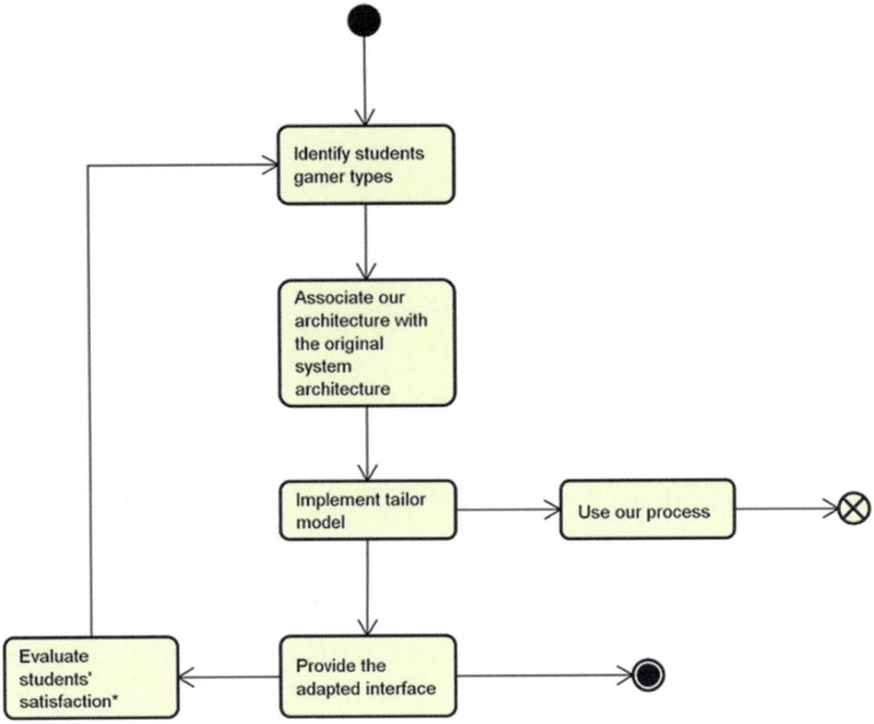

Fig. 5.2 Guideline to adapt TGES based on gamer types

Table 5.4 Most suitable gamification element for each gamer type

Gamer type	Gamification elements					
Achiever	Points	Progress bar	Trophies	Avatars	Badges	
Conqueror	Points	Badges	Levels	Progress bar	Ranking	Avatars
Daredevil	Levels	Trophies	Avatars	Badges	Ranking	
Seeker	Avatars	Badges	Trophies	Points		
Socializer	Points	Ranking	Avatars	Badges	Levels	
Survivor	Avatars	Badges	Ranking			

Table 5.5 Neutral gamification element for each gamer type

Gamer type	Gamification elements				
Achiever	History	Ranking	Levels		
Conqueror	History				
Daredevil	Pointss	Feedback			
Seeker	Progress bar	History	Levels	Feedback	Ranking
Socializer	Feedback	Progress bar	History		
Survivor	Levels	Progress bar	History	Trophies	

Table 5.6 Worst gamification element for each gamer type

Gamer type	Gamification elements		
Achiever	Feedback	Timeline	
Conqueror	Feedback	Timeline	
Daredevil	Timeline	History	Progress bar
Seeker	Timeline		
Socializer	Timeline	Trophies	
Survivor	Points	Timeline	

Fig. 5.3 Gender preference in terms of gamification elements (considering five elements)

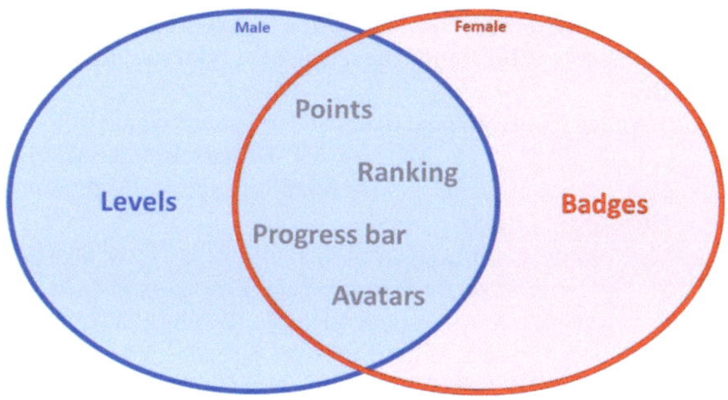

Fig. 5.4 Gender preference in terms of gamification elements (considering three elements)

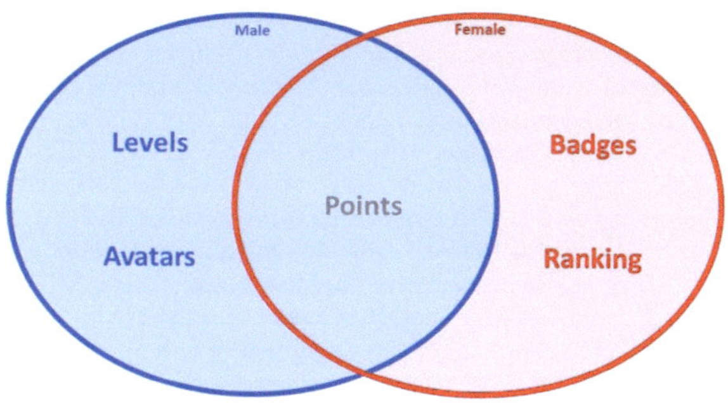

elements, Points, Ranking, Progress bar, and Avatars, may be used for all the students in the system. On the other hand, the gamification element Level should be used only for male students, while the gamification element Badge is more adequate only for female students.

Considering the design for gamified systems with three gamification elements (generally, smaller systems, e.g., educational gamified apps), these elements should be different for both genders, as highlighted in Fig. 5.4. Points might be used for both male and female students. In a tailored system version for the male students, our results suggest using the gamification elements Levels and Avatars. In the tailored system for female students, our results suggest using the elements Badges and Ranking.

References

1. L.E. Nacke, C.S. Deterding, The maturing of gamification research. *Computers in Human Behaviour* (2017), pp. 450–454
2. J. Hamari, J. Koivisto, H. Sarsa, Does gamification work?–A literature review of empirical studies on gamification, in *Proceedings of the 2014 47th Hawaii International Conference on System Sciences (HICSS)* (IEEE, 2014), pp. 3025–3034
3. J. Hamari, D.J. Shernoff, E. Rowe, B. Coller, J. Asbell-Clarke, T. Edwards, Challenging games help students learn: an empirical study on engagement, flow and immersion in game-based learning. Comput. Hum. Behav. **54**, 170–179 (2016)
4. S. Deterding, D. Dixon, R. Khaled, L. Nacke, From game design elements to gamefulness: defining gamification. In *Proceedings of the 15th International Academic MindTrek Conference: Envisioning Future Media Environments* (ACM, 2011). pp. 9–15
5. R. Paharia. Who coined the term. *línea] Quora*. http://goo.gl/CvcMs (2010). Accessed 15 Nov 2017
6. S. Sinha, Motivating students and the gamification of learning. *Huffington Post*, vol. 14 (2012)
7. G.C. Challco, D.A. Moreira, I.I. Bittencourt, R. Mizoguchi, S. Isotani, Personalization of gamification in collaborative learning contexts using ontologies. IEEE Lat. Am. Trans. **13**(6), 1995–2002 (2015)
8. M. Korolov, Gamification of the enterprise. Netw. World **9**(2012), 31–33 (2012)
9. M. Herger, *Enterprise Gamification: Engaging People by Letting Them Have Fun: Book 1-the Basics* (CreateSpace Independent Publishing Platform, 2014)
10. J. Hamari, Do badges increase user activity? A field experiment on the effects of gamification. Comput. Hum. Behav. (2015)
11. S.J. de Santana, H.A. Souza, V.A. Florentin, R. Paiva, I.I. Bittencourt, S. Isotani, A quantitative analysis of the most relevant gamification elements in an online learning environment, in *Proceedings of the 25th International Conference Companion on World Wide Web*. International World Wide Web Conferences Steering Committee (2016), pp. 911–916
12. K. Werbach, (re) defining gamification: a process approach, in *International Conference on Persuasive Technology* (Springer, 2014), pp. 266–272
13. K. Huotari, J. Hamari, "Gamification" from the perspective of service marketing, in *Proceedings of the CHI 2011 Workshop Gamification* (2011)
14. K. Huotari, J. Hamari, A definition for gamification: anchoring gamification in the service marketing literature. Electron. Mark. **27**(1), 21–31 (2017)
15. L.Z. Pedro, A.M. Lopes, B.G. Prates, J. Vassileva, S. Isotani, Does gamification work for boys and girls?: An exploratory study with a virtual learning environment, in *Proceedings of the 30th Annual ACM Symposium on Applied Computing* (ACM, 2015) pp. 214–219
16. D. Dermeval, Authoring gamified intelligent tutoring systems, Ph.D. thesis published on the Federal University of Campina Grande, 2017
17. F.F.-H. Nah, Q. Zeng, V.R. Telaprolu, A.P. Ayyappa, B. Eschenbrenner, Gamification of education: a review of literature, in *Proceedings of the International Conference on HCI in Business* (Springer, 2014), pp. 401–409
18. D. Dicheva, C. Dichev, Gamification in education: where are we in 2015?, in *E-Learn: World Conference on E-Learning in Corporate, Government, Healthcare, and Higher Education*. Association for the Advancement of Computing in Education (AACE) (2015), pp. 1445–1454
19. S. O'Donovan, J. Gain, P. Marais, A case study in the gamification of a university-level games development course, in *Proceedings of the South African Institute for Computer Scientists and Information Technologists Conference* (ACM, 2013), pp. 242–251
20. B. Kumar, P. Khurana, Gamification in education-learn computer programming with fun. Int. J. Comput. Distrib. Syst. **2**(1), 46–53 (2012)
21. G. Goehle, Gamification and web-based homework. Primus **23**(3), 234–246 (2013)
22. M. Alencar, E. Santos, J.F. Netto, Identifying students with evasion risk using data mining, in *EdMedia: World Conference on Educational Media and Technology*. Association for the Advancement of Computing in Education (AACE) (2015), pp. 611–616

23. R. Brewer, L. Anthony, Q. Brown, G. Irwin, J. Nias, B. Tate, Using gamification to motivate children to complete empirical studies in lab environments, in *Proceedings of the 12th International Conference on Interaction Design and Children* (ACM, 2013), pp. 388–391
24. R. Raymer, Gamification: using game mechanics to enhance elearning. eLearn **2011**(9), 3 (2011)
25. K. Berkling, C. Thomas, Gamification of a software engineering course and a detailed analysis of the factors that lead to it's failure, in *2013 International Conference on Interactive Collaborative Learning (ICL)* (IEEE, 2013). pp. 525–530
26. K.M. Kapp, Games, gamification, and the quest for learner engagement. T+ D **66**(6), 64–68 (2012)
27. M. Csikszentmihalyi, *Beyond Boredom and Anxiety* (Jossey-Bass, 2000)
28. M. Csikszentmihalyi, *Finding Flow: The Psychology of Engagement with Everyday Life* (Basic Books, 1997)
29. V.R.B.-G. Caldiera, H.D. Rombach, Goal question metric paradigm. Encycl. Softw. Eng. **1**, 528–532 (1994)
30. P.M. Stohr-Hunt, An analysis of frequency of hands-on experience and science achievement. J. Res. Sci. Teach.: Official J. Natl. Assoc. Res. Sci. Teach. **33**(1), 101–109 (1996)
31. R. Van Solingen, E. Berghout, *The Goal/Question/Metric Method: A Practical Guide for Quality Improvement of Software Development* (McGraw-Hill, 1999)
32. R. Likert, A technique for the measurement of attitudes. Arch. Psychol. (1932)
33. R. Delgado, Storytelling for oppositionists and others: a plea for narrative. Mich. Law Rev. **87**(8), 2411–2441 (1989)
34. G.F. Tondello, A. Mora, L.E. Nacke, Elements of gameful design emerging from user preferences, in *Proceedings of the Annual Symposium on Computer-Human Interaction in Play* (ACM, 2017), pp. 129–142
35. D. Codish, G. Ravid, Gender moderation in gamification: does one size fit all? (2017)
36. A. Khan, F.H. Ahmad, M.M. Malik, Use of digital game based learning and gamification in secondary school science: the effect on student engagement, learning and gender difference. Educ. Inf. Technol. **22**(6), 2767–2804 (2017)
37. D.C. Howell, *Statistical Methods for Psychology* (Cengage Learning, 2012)
38. J.W. Tukey, Comparing individual means in the analysis of variance. Biometrics 99–114 (1949)
39. T.K. Kim, T test as a parametric statistic. Korean J. Anesthesiol. **68**(6), 540–546 (2015)
40. A. Mora, D. Riera, C. González, J. Arnedo-Moreno, Gamification: a systematic review of design frameworks. J. Comput. High. Educ. **29**(3), 516–548 (2017)
41. J. Hamari, J. Tuunanen, Player types: a meta-synthesis. Trans. Digit. Games Res. Assoc. **1**(2) (2014)

Chapter 6
MeuTutor: Personalizing an Educational Technology Based on Students' Gamer Types

Abstract In the last few years, different types of educational systems have been developed with different objectives, such as helping students prepare for assessments, helping large groups of students to graduate or even specialize at a distance, and even helping students learn a new language. In this chapter, in order to present in a practical way an approach to tailor gamified educational systems in a real scenario, we will present the tailored gamification design process of a gamified educational system called *MeuTutor*. The system was developed in Brazil and has already helped over 10,000 elementary and high school students to study and learn in a fun and motivating way. This chapter will begin by presenting the original gamified educational system design, before the tailoring process. It will present, as well, how the tailoring process was conducted and the final result, showing the tailored version of the system. We will also present in this chapter, an evaluation of the system, comparing the tailored and counter-tailored version of the system in terms of students' concentration. In the end, a series of lessons learned throughout the tailoring process and system evaluation will be presented.

6.1 Original Gamification Design

MeuTutor® is a Brazilian gamified educational system, developed to provide the teachers with an environment capable of elaborating and sharing different learning materials, such as: videos, hypertexts, questionnaires, evaluations, and others. It also provides the students with activities associated with gamification elements, with the objective to produce a ludic and motivational learning process. *MeuTutor*®, according to [1], also aims to offer personalized support for each student.

MeuTutor® provides a series of gamification elements that were chosen to be used in the original (counter-tailored) version, according to a series of studies related to gamification elements applied to education and its consequences for students' learning *e.g.*, [2–4]. The main gamification elements used in *MeuTutor*®, as well as the description of each element, are organized on the Table 6.1.

The tailoring process and architectural design for the gamified educational system based on gamer types were implemented in this system. The system was chosen after a

W. Oliveira and I. I. Bittencourt, *Tailored Gamification to Educational Technologies*,
https://doi.org/10.1007/978-981-32-9812-5_6

Table 6.1 *MeuTutor*® gamification elements

Game element	Description
1- Points (XP)	*MeuTutor*® provides to the students' Experience Points (XP) according to their participation in the activities proposed by the system, with each activity executed by the students (e.g., view a video or response a question) generating Points for them
2- Levels/stages	*MeuTutor*® provides to the students a series of levels/stages according to the chosen course and topics defined by the professor. Initially, the student has only the first levels/stages "opened" and the next levels/stage unlocked depending on their performance
3- Badges	*MeuTutor*® provides different Badges to the students through their experience into the systems, with these Badges being provided when the students complete a proposed activity, such as watching a series of videos and responding a questionnaire about a determined topic correctly, among others
4- Leaderboards	*MeuTutor*® provides to the students a Leaderboard with their amount of Points and place in the system, as well as the number of Points and place of their main "opponents"
5- Trophies	*MeuTutor*® provides to the students prizes and rewards at each completed level/stage
6- Progress bars	*MeuTutor*® provides to the students a Progress bar according to their performance in the system. The Progress bar increases with each activity completed by the student
7- Storyline	*MeuTutor*® provides to the students a storyline in the form of a calendar, so the students can see their evolution in the system, from their first activities until their current stage
8- Feedback	*MeuTutor*® provides to the students a feedback according to their performance in each activity. In this sense, for each activity where the student makes a mistake, he will receive a feedback with an explanation about the related question
9- Ranking and leaderboards	*MeuTutor*® provides a Ranking with Leaderboards based on the students' performance in the system
10- Background history	*MeuTutor*® provides five different background histories to be chosen in the students' first access in the system
11- Avatar	*MeuTutor*® provides five different Avatars associated with each background stories before they are addressed

comparative analysis among different gamified educational systems. *MeuTutor*® was of interest for us because it was considered more geographically accessible, as well as implemented the nine most used gamification elements in gamified educational systems, as identified by Nah et al. [5] and Dicheva and Dicheva [6], which avoided some validity threats. We will present next the complete process to tailor the system: starting with the students' gamer type identification, continuing with the selection of gamification elements, and finishing with different versions of the system, with the specific gamification elements to each gamer type.

Fig. 6.1 Avatar choice and story background

6.1.1 Requirements Engineering

The tailoring process was done in terms of graphical interface, changing the gamification design model (game design elements), according to the students' gamer type, and based on the proposed approach in Chap. 4. To identify the student's gamer type, the *BrainHex* questionnaire was attached to the system [7]. After the students answered the *BrainHex* questionnaire, they also immediately received their gamer type, with some information about it (according to the *BrainHex* study). The students were asked if they agreed or not with their gamer type, like the original *BrainHex* questionnaire.

We used the PHP programming languages (which originally stood for Personal Home Page, but now stands for the recursive acronym PHP: Hypertext Preprocessor); HTML (HyperText Markup Language); standard markup language for creating web pages and web applications; and CSS (Cascading Style Sheets); the style sheet language used for describing the presentation of a document written in a markup language. To test the tailoring process, a local server named XAMPP was used, a free and open-source web server with a cross-platform solution stack package.

The original system (with default game design elements) is composed of six different screens: *(i)* the chosen Avatar and background, *(ii)* homepage, *(ii)* tree of activities, *(iv)* individual activity, *(v)* exercise, and *(vi)* student's profile. In the first moment (first access on the system), the students can choose their Avatar (among five different options (two male, two female, and one neutral)), and a story associated with the Avatar (Fig. 6.1 presents this screen).

In the second moment, after choosing the Avatar, the student can access the system homepage. In this screen, the student can access their courses or see their profile.

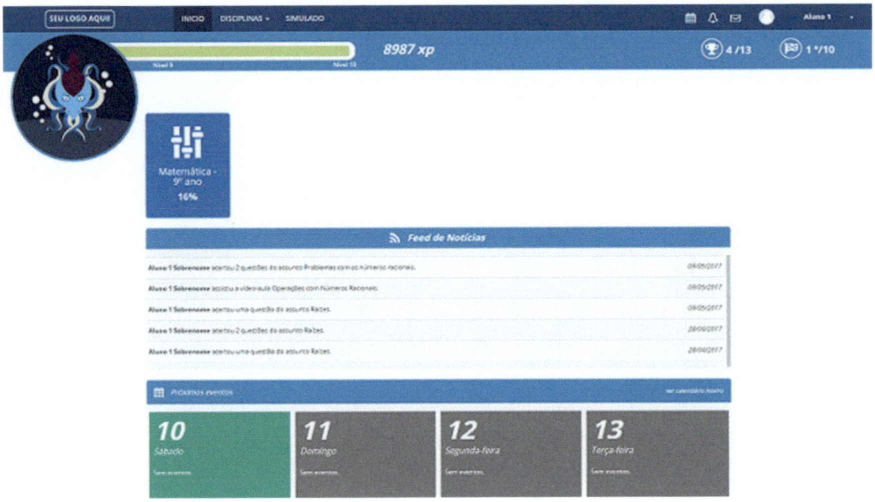

Fig. 6.2 System home page

This screen presents the game design elements Points, Trophies, Ranking, Progress Bar, and Timeline (Fig. 6.2 presents this screen).

In the third screen, the student can access the tree of activities (associated with the gamification element *evolution*) with the available activities. This screen presents the game design element Progress Bar (see Fig. 6.3). Initially, only the first activity is released in the system for student' access. Only after the student finishes the first activity, the following activities will be accessible. This is because activities in general are dependent, as well as associated with the element of gamification "Level."

After choosing a specific activity, in the fourth screen, the student has access to the activity, like, for instance: watching a video, answering a questionnaire, among others. This screen presents the gamification elements Progress Bar and Badges (see Fig. 6.4), and after that, the student can access a specific exercise related to the topic chosen before. When performing an activity, the students also receive an automatic feedback of their performance in the activity, as well as have access to tips related to the activity that they are doing.

Finally, in the sixth screen, the students access their profile and have the option to change their profile picture, nickname, etc. This screen organizes the game design elements: Points, Level (associated with the Progress Bar), Ranking (with Leaderboards), and Trophies (Fig. 6.5). All gamification design and overall system design was developed by several specialists in CHI, assessed and validated in recent studies [2–4].

Fig. 6.3 System activities tree

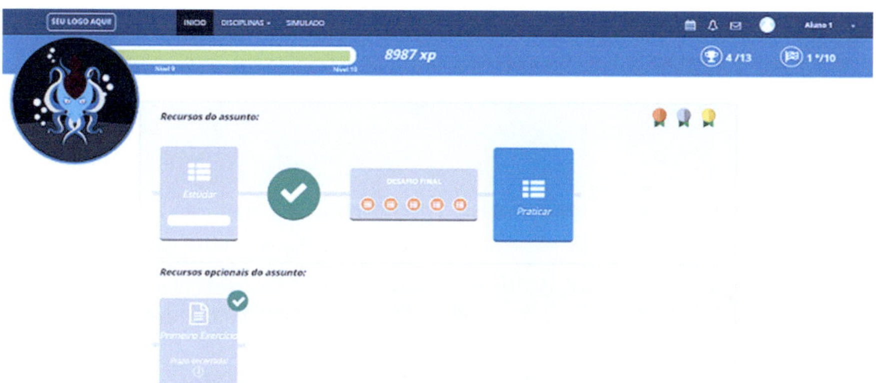

Fig. 6.4 System activities

6.1.2 Authoring Prototyping

In the tailoring process, we first associated the original system architectural design with our approach. This was important for the association of the gamification elements to each *BrainHex* gamer type. Afterward, we implemented a tailored model, taking the gamification elements provided by the system and associating these gamification elements to each student gamer type. Finally, we identified the students'

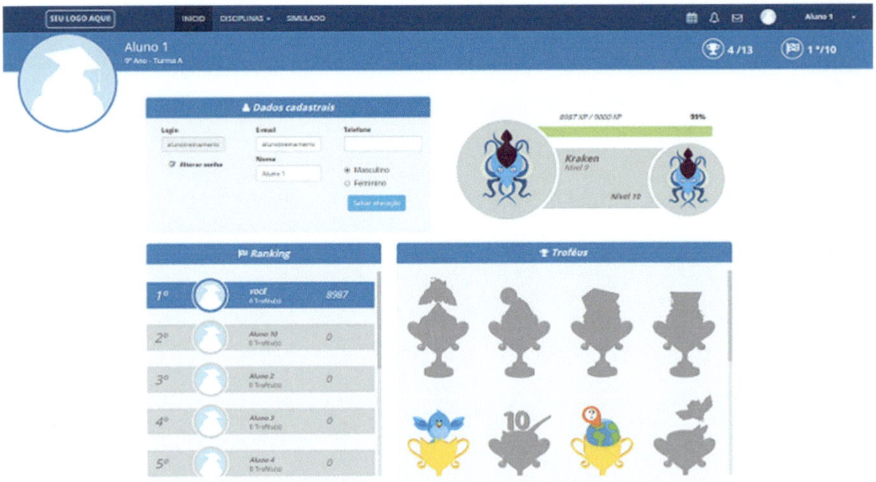

Fig. 6.5 System profile

gamer types using the *BrainHex* reference and provided the different versions of the system, with the adapted interface to each group of students.

6.1.3 Architectural Design and Implementation

After the tailoring process, the **Achiever students'** interface was changed according to the proposed approach (Chap. 4 of this book), as it follows: *(i)* the Avatar choice and story background were removed from the first screen; *(ii)* the Progress Bar, Timeline, and Ranking were removed from the home page; *(iii)* the Ranking (with Leaderboards) and Levels (with Progress Bar) were removed from the student's profile. On the other hand, the Points and Trophies were kept on the homepage, and the Badges were kept on the activities screen. The profile kept only the gamification element Trophies (see Appendix A: Figs. A.1, A.2, and A.3).

The **Conqueror students'** interface was changed as it follows: *(i)* the Progress Bar, Points, and Trophies were removed from the homepage, and *(ii)* the Progress bar, Levels, and Trophies were removed from the profile. On the other hand, the Avatar choice and adapted story background were kept on the first access, the Timeline and Ranking (with Leaderboards) were kept on the homepage, and the Badges were also kept on the screen of activities. The profile kept only the Ranking (with Leaderboards) (see Appendix A: Figs. A.4, A.5, and A.6).

In the **Daredevil students'** interface *(i)* the Points, Trophies, and Timeline were removed from the homepage; *(ii)* Badges were removed from the activities page; and *(iii)* Levels and Trophies were also removed from the profile page. On the other hand, the Avatar choice and adapted story background were kept on the first access, and the Ranking (with Leaderboards) was kept on the homepage. The profile kept only the Ranking (with Leaderboards) and Progress Bar (see Appendix A: Figs. A.7, A.8, and A.9).

The **Mastermind students'** interface was changed, so, *(i)* Trophies and Timeline were removed from the homepage, and *(ii)* Levels and Trophies were also removed from the profile page. On the other hand, the Avatar choice and adapted story background were kept on the first access; Points, Progress Bar, and Ranking (with Leaderboards) were kept on the homepage, and the Badges were kept on the activities page. The profile kept the Ranking (with Leaderboards) and Progress Bar (see Appendix A: Figs. A.10, A.11, and A.12).

After the tailoring process, the **Seeker students'** interface was changed, as it follows: *(i)* the Avatar choice and adapted story background were removed from first access; *(ii)* Ranking with Leaderboards; and *(iii)* Prizes to be chosen. In this case, the Seeker students must select the Prizes. For instance, when the Seeker student wins a Trophy, they can choose a specific Trophy to their collection of prizes. In this case, we will not present the personal interface of this gamer type because it follows a design similar to that of the original system, giving the student the option to choose their own prizes

In the **Socializer students'** interface *(i)* the the Avatar choice and adapted story background were removed from first access; *(ii)* the Timeline, Progress bar, Points, and Trophies were removed from home page; *(iii)* the badges were removed from activities page; and *(iv)* the levels, Progress bar, and Trophies were removed from profile page. In this profile, the system kept only the Ranking with Leaderboards. (see Appendix A: Figs. A.13, A.14, and A.15).

In the **Survivor students'** interface *(i)* also, the Avatar choice and adapted story background were removed from first access; *(ii)* the Timeline and Trophies were removed from the home page; *(iii)* the Badges were removed from the activities page; and *(iv)* Level and Trophies were removed from the profile page. On the other hand, Points, Progress Bar, and Ranking with Leaderboards were kept on the home page and profile. The tailored screens for each game type can be found in the appendices of this book. (see Appendix A: Figs. A.16, A.17, and A.18).

6.2 Evaluating the System

To evaluate the quality of the system, we conducted an experiment comparing the tailored and counter-tailored version of the gamified educational system with 121 Brazilian students in terms of students' concentration. In the experiment, the students used the two versions of the system (a randomness algorithm was used to define which of the versions the student would use first). Following, we will present details about the experiment.

6.2.1 Research Question and Hypothesis

In order to conduct the experiment, the following research question was proposed:

RQ1. Is the tailored system based on the students' gamer types more effective to lead the students into concentration during the activities compared to the counter-tailored system?

According to the research question previously presented, we defined the following hypothesis:

$H_1 \cdot_0$: The Achiever students' concentration in the tailored system is less than or equal to the Achiever students' concentration in the counter-tailored system.

$H_1 \cdot_1$: The Achiever students' concentration in the tailored system is greater than the achiever students' concentration in the counter-tailored system.

$H_2 \cdot_0$: The Conqueror students' concentration in the tailored system is less than or equal to the Conqueror students' concentration in the counter-tailored system.

$H_2 \cdot_1$: The Conqueror students' concentration in the tailored system is greater than the conqueror students' concentration in the counter-tailored system.

$H_3 \cdot_0$: The Daredevil students' concentration in the tailored system is less than or equal to the Daredevil students' concentration in the counter-tailored system.

$H_3 \cdot_1$: The Daredevil students' concentration in the tailored system is greater than the Daredevil students' concentration in the counter-tailored system.

$H_4 \cdot_0$: The Mastermind students' concentration in the tailored system is less than or equal to the Mastermind students' concentration in the counter-tailored system.

$H_4 \cdot_1$: The Mastermind students' concentration in the tailored system is greater than the Mastermind students' concentration in the counter-tailored system.

$H_5 \cdot_0$: The Seeker students' concentration in the tailored system is less than or equal to the Seeker students' concentration in the counter-tailored system.

$H_5 \cdot_1$: The Seeker students' concentration in the tailored system is greater than the Seeker students' concentration in the counter-tailored system.

$H_6 \cdot_0$: The Socializer students' concentration in the tailored system is less than or equal to the Socializer students' concentration in the counter-tailored system.

$H_6 \cdot_1$: The Socializer students' concentration in the tailored system is greater than the Socializer students' concentration in the counter-tailored system.

$H_7 \cdot_0$: The Survivor students' concentration in the tailored system is less than or equal to the Survivor students' concentration in the counter-tailored system.

$H_7 \cdot_1$: The Survivor students' concentration in the tailored system is greater than the Survivor Students' concentration in the counter-tailored system.

The formal definition of the hypothesis has the objective to organize the hypothesis in a mathematical formulation. Table 6.2 organizes our formal hypothesis definition.

6.2.1.1 Factors, Response Variables, and Experimental Unities

According to the hypothesis previously defined, our experiment has one factor, the gamified system with two levels (tailored and counter-tailored version). The response

Table 6.2 Formal definition of the hypothesis

Hypothesis	Null hypothesis	Alternative hypothesis
H_1	H_0: E (TS (Ac)) ≤ E (cTS (Ac))	H_1: E (TS (Ac)) > E (cTS (Ac))
H_2	H_0: E (TS (Cn)) ≤ E (cTS (Cn))	H_1: E (TS (Cn)) > E (cTS (Cn))
H_3	H_0: E (TS (Dr)) ≤ E (cTS (Dr))	H_1: E (TS (Dr)) > E (cTS (Dr))
H_4	H_0: E (TS (Ms)) ≤ E (cTS (Ms))	H_1: E (TS (Ms)) > E (cTS (Ms))
H_5	H_0: E (TS (Sk)) ≤ E (cTS (Sk))	H_1: E (TS (Sk)) > E (cTS (Sk))
H_6	H_0: E (TS (Ss)) ≤ E (cTS (Ss))	H_1: E (TS (Ss)) > E (cTS (Ss))
H_7	H_0: E (TS (Sv)) ≤ E (cTS (Sv))	H_1: E (TS (Sv)) > E (cTS (Sv))

Key: Ac: Achiever, Cn: Conqueror, Dr: Daredevil, Ms: Mastermind, Sk: Seeker, Ss: Socializer, Sv: Survivor, E: Concentration, TS: Tailored System, cTS: Counter-tailored System

Table 6.3 Sample of experiment

Gamer type	Sample	Male	Female
Achiever	48	18	30
Conqueror	28	15	12
Daredevil	6	5	1
Mastermind	3	0	3
Seeker	16	5	11
Socializer	9	5	4
Survivor	12	4	8
Total	**121**	**52**	**69**

variable is the students' concentration. We defined a metric to measure these preferences in partnership with two academic professionals with expertise in Statistical and Behavioral Science. This metric is an average between 1 and 5 according to the students' answers regarding their concentration. Our experimental unities are our sample composed of elementary students (organized according to their gamer types) interacting with gamified systems.

6.2.2 Participants

We collected data from 121 Brazilian middle school students, in which 52 were male and 69 were female, aged between 11 and 13 years (with an average age of 12 years old). Table 6.3 presents details about our sample.

6.2.3 Data Collection and Metrics Definition

The research data was stored using pseudonym and association with questionnaire data and data logs. The data was stored in a password-protected computer system to be accessed only by the investigators. A secure cabinet was used to store the data for the long term. The experiment was conducted in a controlled environment (a laboratory with 20 computers with Windows 7 installed and free access to the internet). First, the students responded to the *BrainHex* questionnaire to identify their gamer type.

In the second step, students were organized in seven different groups according to their gamer types; each group of students was randomly divided into two different groups (experimental and control group) to use the system (static version). In the third step, the students of the experimental group used the tailored version for their gamer type and, in the sequence, responded to the scale to measure concentration. At the same time, the control group used the counter-tailored version and also responded the scale. Next, the experimental group repeated the same process using the counter-tailored system and the control group used the tailored system.

In the fourth step, the students' answers were organized in tables (*.csv* files) and separated according to each gamer type and the version of the system (tailored and counter-tailored version), like the concentration of the students in the tailored and counter-tailored version. In the fifth step, the answers were organized, according to the original scale factorial structure validated by [8]. Then, we calculated the individual and general way in which each concentration and flow experience was built.

Finally, in the sixth step, we calculated the metrics defined (see next section) in order to compare the difference in terms of concentration for the seven different gamer types in the tailored and in the counter-tailored version of the system.

The metrics were extracted through the analysis of data previously collected, using different statistical software tools and the application of different statistical tests. In order to identify the students' concentration, we used the part of the Dispositional Flow Scale-2 (DFS-2) [8]. The DFS-2 scale consists of structures based on the nine Flow Theory dimensions defined by [9], and empirically validated for the gamification domain by [8]. In this experiment, we used only the four questions concerning students' concentration measurement. Therefore, the items were measured on a Likert scale ranging from strong disagreement (1 on the Likert scale) to strong agreement (5 on the Likert scale) toward the statement.

In order to investigate the concentration differences of each gamer type in each version of the implemented system, we calculated the mean, median, standard deviation, average variation, maximum shared variation, average shared variation, and normality of the data. Finally, based on the normality of data, we calculated the variance analyses between the students' concentration in the tailored and in the counter-tailored version of the system for each gamer type. The data of the preferences metric is normal; hence, we decided to apply the *t-test* to verify the hypothesis. The application of the test, considering a $p \leq 0.05$ level of significance with 95% confidence level.

Table 6.4 Students' concentration

	Counter-tailored system				Tailored system			
μ	~x	σ	$var(X)$	μ	~x	σ	$var(X)$	*t-test*
Achiver								
3.600	3.625	0.905	0.819	3.595	3.750	0.798	0.637	0.976
Conqueror								
3.775	3.875	0.889	0.790	3.817	3.875	0.833	0.694	0.852
Daredevil								
2.950	2.750	1.022	1.044	3.200	3.250	1.037	1.075	0.711
Mastermind								
3.250	3.250	0.612	0.375	3.438	3.500	0.944	0.891	0.752
Seeker								
4.143	4.125	0.663	0.440	3.964	4.250	0.980	0.960	0.577
Socializer								
3.865	4.000	0.704	0.496	3.583	3.500	0.606	0.367	0.293
Survivor								
3.550	3.375	0.848	0.719	3.800	4.250	0.949	0.900	0.542

Key: μ = Mean, ~x = Median, σ = Standard deviation, $var(X)$ = Average variation, AOV = Variance analysis

6.2.4 Results

Table 6.4 presents the complete result of our analysis for each gamer type using the tailored and counter-tailored versions of the system.

By analyzing the individual results obtained for each gamer type, it is possible to perceive that in general, the Achiever students' concentration was similar in both versions of the system (counter-tailored version = 3.600 – tailored version = 3.595), which means that the students' concentration in the tailored version was not bigger than the students' concentration in the counter-tailored version. The t-test results (*p-value* = 0.976) also confirm that there was no statistically significant difference between the students' concentration in the tailored version in comparison with the counter-tailored version. So, we did not reject our null hypothesis.

For the Conquerors, the concentration was better in the tailored version of the system compared to the counter-tailored systems (counter-tailored version = 3.775 – tailored version = 3.817). Although the concentration was higher in the personalized version of the system, the statistic test indicated that this difference was not statistically significant (*p-value* = 0.852). So, once again, we did not reject our null hypothesis for the Conqueror's concentration.

The Daredevil students presented a difference in terms of concentration. Similar to the Achievers and Conquerors, the Daredevil's concentration was better in the tailored system (counter-tailored version = 2.950 – tailored version = 3.200). For the Daredevil students' concentration, the t-test also indicated that the difference was not statistically significant (*p-value* = 0.711) and we did not reject our null hypothesis.

The Masterminds presented positive difference in terms of concentration in the tailored version of the system. For this gamer type, the concentration in the counter-tailored version was 3.250 and in the tailored version was 3.438. The t-test indicated a *p-value* equal to 0.752, indicating that the difference identified was not statistically significant. For this gamer type, we also did not reject our null hypothesis.

The Seekers' concentration was higher in the counter-tailored version of the system (counter-tailored version = 4.143—tailored version = 3.964). The statistic test conducted resulted in a *p-value* equal to 0.577, indicating that although the concentration was higher in the non-personalized system, the difference was not significant. So, for this case, we also did not reject our null hypothesis.

In terms of concentration, the experience of the Socializer students' was higher in the counter-tailored system (counter-tailored version = 3.865—tailored version = 3.583) and the t-test returned the *p-value* 0.293. Then, we did not reject our null hypothesis about the Socializer students' concentration.

Finally, the concentration of the Survivor students was better in the tailored system (counter-tailored version = 3.550 - tailored version = 3.800). After we executed the t-test, the result (*p-value* = 0.542) indicated that for this gamer type, the difference also was not statistically significant. So we also did not reject our null hypothesis about the Survivor students' concentration.

6.2.5 *Threats to Validity*

This section presents some concerns to be discussed in possible replications of this study and some points that must be considered in order to maximize the finds of the performed evaluation. We tried to minimize the presented threats in this chapter. To organize this section, the validity threats were organized using the **Internal**, **External**, **Construct**, and **Conclusion** categories of Wohlin [10].

Internal: our experiment was carried out with real users, which could generate the following threats: *(i)* history—it is possible that at the time the experiment happened, the environment may have affected participants' experience, but this limitation was minimized by through the freedom of use given to the participants, who could use the system without influence of the teachers or other participants; *(ii)* maturation—since the participants first had to use the system for about 30 min and then respond to a questionnaire, users might have been tired when they started responding to the questionnaire; and *(iii)* positive or negative bias—as most of the participants do not have experience in this type of evaluation, they may have been nervous about using the system and answering the questionnaire. To minimize this threat, the two versions of the system (tailor and counter-tailored) were evaluated by the students in different moments.

External: In this study, the sample is more representative for the academic domain. As before explained, the students that participated in our study were elementary school students. Thus, we might not be able to maximize our results of this experiment into different contexts. The subjects of this evaluation should be expanded to other academic settings to obtain more generic results.

Constructs: In this category, the threats are related to two aspects of the study. This study measures different aspects and some constructs maybe not be identified by the questions. To minimize these threats, we selected methodologies and instruments validated and oftentimes used in experimental studies from the technological and educational field. The system used in this experiment has an interface design (in terms of gamification elements), so the students' experience in the system can be influenced by the system design beyond the gamification elements.

Conclusion: The sample size of this experiment was of 121 students. However, this was a blocking factorial experiment, and some groups may have a small sample to confirm some hypothesis. The elementary students that were participants of the experiment could have been anxious at the moment that they answered the questionnaire, and they may have answered it without the proper attention. To mitigate this, we used only instruments previously validated in different domains, including gamification domains.

6.3 Lessons Learned

After the implementation of the system with a tailored gamification design and its evaluation, different lessons were learned. It was possible to identify that all of the gamer types did not have a significant statistical difference in terms of concentration in the tailored and in the counter-tailored systems. For some gamer types, the tailored system was better than the counter-tailored system, showing that students can be more motivated for educational systems tailored according to their gamification preferences.

However, our results, in some cases, surprised the expectations of the communities, contradicting some recent studies conducted in this field (i.e., [11–13] and others). It indicated that the students' concentration was better in the counter-tailored system. On the one hand, this may show that TGES may not be effective for all situations; on the other hand, this result may also indicate failures in the system design process.

A series of contribution was obtained from these results, for instance, the literature presents some initial studies about systems personalization based on gamer types; however, our study is the first or one of first specifically conducted to the field of education, in other words, considering this domain, the results can be different in other domains. Our results also open a series of discussions about the educational system's personalization, and about how to tailor gamified educational systems for better motivating each student gamer type.

Regardless of that, our results indicate that the process used to implement the tailored system is capable of tailoring gamified intelligent educational systems based on students' gamer types. Also, the tailored and counter-tailored versions of the system had different influences on the students' experience. At the same time, the results indicate that this is an open research field, that needs to receive more empirical studies, in order to investigate important things. For instance, to conduct experimental studies in order to investigate which are the best persuasive strategies and provide evaluations in terms of CHI in tailored and counter-TGES.

References

1. R.O.A. Paiva, I.I. Bittencourt, A.P. da Silva, S. Isotani, P. Jaques, Improving pedagogical recommendations by classifying students according to their interactional behavior in a gamified learning environment, in *Proceedings of the 30th Annual ACM Symposium on Applied Computing*, pp. 233–238. ACM (2015)
2. R. Paiva, A. Barbosa, E. Batista, D. Pimentel, I.I. Bittencourt, Badges and XP: an observational study about learning, in *2015 IEEE Frontiers in Education Conference (FIE)*, pp. 1–8. IEEE (2015)
3. R. Paiva, I.I. Bittencourt, T. Tenório, P. Jaques, S. Isotani, What do students do on-line? modeling students' interactions to improve their learning experience. Comput. Hum. Behav. **64**, 769–781 (2016)
4. G.C. Challco, R. Mizoguchi, I.I. Bittencourt, S. Isotani, Gamification of collaborative learning scenarios: structuring persuasive strategies using game elements and ontologies, in *International Workshop on Social Computing in Digital Education*, pp. 12–28. Springer (2015)
5. F.F-H. Nah, Q. Zeng, V.R. Telaprolu, A.P. Ayyappa, B. Eschenbrenner, Gamification of education: a review of literature, in *International Conference on HCI in Business*, pp. 401–409. Springer (2014)
6. D. Dicheva, C. Dichev, Gamification in education: where are we in 2015? in *E-Learn: World Conference on E-Learning in Corporate, Government, Healthcare, and Higher Education*, pp. 1445–1454. Association for the Advancement of Computing in Education (AACE) (2015)
7. L.E. Nacke, C. Bateman, R.L. Mandryk, Brainhex: a neurobiological gamer typology survey. Entertain. Comput. **5**(1), 55–62 (2014)
8. J. Hamari, J. Koivisto, Measuring flow in gamification: dispositional flow scale-2. Comput. Hum. Behav. **40**, 133–143 (2014)
9. M. Csikszentmihalyi, *Finding Flow: The Psychology of Engagement with Everyday Life* (Basic Books, New York, 1997)
10. C. Wohlin, P. Runeson, M. Höst, M. C. Ohlsson, B. Regnell, A. Wesslén, *Experimentation in Software Engineering* (Springer Science & Business Media, Berlin, 2012)
11. R. Orji, R.L. Mandryk, J. Vassileva, K.M. Gerling, Tailoring persuasive health games to gamer type, in *Proceedings of the SIGCHI Conference on Human Factors in Computing Systems*, pp. 2467–2476. ACM (2013)
12. R. Orji, R.L. Mandryk, J. Vassileva, Selecting effective strategies for tailoring persuasive health games to gamer types (2014)
13. B. Monterrat, É. Lavoué, S. George, Toward an adaptive gamification system for learning environments, in *International Conference on Computer Supported Education*, pp. 115–129. Springer (2014)

Chapter 7
Conclusions

Abstract Although we know the limitations related to the application of gamification in educational systems, there are still few studies that seek to investigate these limitations and provide solutions for them. One of the most striking limitations in recent years is that most of the gamified educational systems use the same gamification elements for all users, with no respect for possible individualities and preferences on the part of the users. Thus, throughout this book, we led a series of studies related to the investigation of how the students perceive the gamification design of the gamified educational systems according to their particularities, as well as proposed solutions for the personalization of this type of system. Finally, in this final chapter, we intend to synthesize the results of this book, presenting a series of challenges, opportunities, and research directions related to the personalization of gamification in educational environments.

7.1 Traveled Paths

One of the main challenges related to the design of educational systems is to provide good environments to the students, capable to keep them engaged, concentrated and motivated during their activities, and also increase their learning performance [1–3]. With the objective of increasing the students' motivation in this kind of system, the gamification tool has been widely used in different perspectives [4].

Besides, gamification presented good results in different studies, like, for instance, keeping the students motivated during the activities provided by the system or improving the students' engagement [1, 5, 6]. On the other hand, other studies showed that gamification can cause the opposite effect [7–9]. One of the main hypothesis to this situation is that students have different styles (for instance, different gamer types) and are motivated by different gamification elements, according to their style.

In order to investigate and discuss these problems, we conducted different studies with the objective to investigate whether students have different preferences with respect to the gamification design according to its style and provide an approach to tailor gamified educational systems based on diverse characteristics. We implemented seven different versions of a gamified educational system using the proposed

W. Oliveira and I. I. Bittencourt, *Tailored Gamification to Educational Technologies*,
https://doi.org/10.1007/978-981-32-9812-5_7

approach and conducted a comparative evaluation in terms of concentration with the students using a tailored and counter-tailored version of the system.

The main general findings presented in this book indicates that for some gamer types, the tailored system was more effective in terms of concentration in comparison with the counter-tailored system, confirming our expectations and recent studies in this field. On the other hand, the same study also indicates that for other gamer types, the counter-tailored system was more effective than the tailored system, which shows that new studies need to be conducted to further investigate these results.

Concerning our investigation about whether students have different preferences on gamification elements according to their style, the main results confirmed that the students have different perceptions according to their gamer type and confirmed most of the recent studies in this field in terms of which are the best gamification elements for each gamer type. The results also showed some new perspectives in terms of gamification elements preferences of the different students' gamer type. The guideline provided through these results can be used by different professional types to identify the best gamification elements to each gamer type.

7.1.1 Challenges, Opportunities, and Research Direction on Tailored Gamification to Educational Technologies

According to the results of the different studies presented in this book, we aim to propose at this moment some challenges that can be investigated in the next years and recommend some possibilities to solve these challenges. Initially, we think it is important to recommend for future studies to associate more gamification elements and game mechanics with each *BrainHex* gamer type (or other player model). It may provide a deeper view regarding the motivational items for each gamer type and conduct different kinds of evaluations in different versions of the tailored system based on the students' gamer types, gender, age, and others, including investigating different constructs, such as the students' motivation and engagement, and with different subjects samples (i.e., gamification designers).

Further, one problem in regard to the personalization of gamified educational systems is that it is generally necessary for the students to fill out some questionnaire where, over time, it is possible for the student to change their profile. Hence, the system is not able to identify this change unless it routinely applies the questionnaire. In this sense, an important challenge related to personalization of gamification design in the educational system is to provide an automatic tailoring process, without the need for questionnaires or invasive equipment, such as electroencephalogram (EEG) or eye tracker.

Given this, the use of resources based on artificial intelligence appears as a viable opportunity to face this challenge [10]. Currently, several resources related to artificial integrity can be used for this purpose. One of these possibilities is the use of statistical techniques to give computer systems the ability to "learn" (e.g., progressively improve performance on a specific task) from data, without being explicitly programmed. Other similar possibility is the use of data miming, that is, the process of discovering patterns in large data sets involving methods at the intersection of machine learning, statistics, and database systems. Besides these, another young possibility is the learning analytics, that is the measurement, collection, analysis, and reporting of data about learners and their contexts, for purposes of understanding and optimizing learning and the environments in which it occurs.

All of these options corroborate the automatic collection of data (without the need for questionnaires or the aforementioned equipment), analysis of these data, and identification of possible patterns of student behavior, which may indicate, for example, a particular gamer type, or the exchange of a gamer type for another during the interaction with the system. Thus, based on this information, it is possible to make the gamified educational system design change automatically according to each student. Also, with these techniques, it is possible to provide an implicit evaluation of the quality of the system in terms of students' perception about the system gamification design.

We also cannot forget to think of gamification on a broader level, seeking not only a change in the level of gamification elements, but to extend personalization to the whole design of the system, including seeking to link personalization of gamification with the personalization of the system interface design and pedagogical design, so as to think more directly about the personalization based on the multiple characteristics and singularities of the students.

References

1. S.J. de Santana, H.A. Souza, V.A. Florentin, R. Paiva, I.I. Bittencourt, S. Isotani, A quantitative analysis of the most relevant gamification elements in an online learning environment, in *Proceedings of the 25th International Conference Companion on World Wide Web*, pp. 911–916. International World Wide Web Conferences Steering Committee (2016)
2. J. Hamari, D.J. Shernoff, E. Rowe, B. Coller, J. Asbell-Clarke, T. Edwards, Challenging games help students learn: an empirical study on engagement, flow and immersion in game-based learning. Comput. Hum. Behav. **54**, 170–179 (2016)
3. D. Janßen, C. Tummel, A. Richert, I. Isenhardt, Towards measuring user experience, activation and task performance in immersive virtual learning environments for students, in *International Conference on Immersive Learning* (Springer, 2016), pp. 45–58
4. J. Hamari, J. Koivisto, H. Sarsa, Does gamification work?–a literature review of empirical studies on gamification, in *2014 47th Hawaii International Conference on System Sciences (HICSS)* (IEEE, 2014), pp. 3025–3034
5. R.O.A. Paiva, I.I. Bittencourt, A.P. da Silva, S. Isotani, P. Jaques, Improving pedagogical recommendations by classifying students according to their interactional behavior in a gamified learning environment, in *Proceedings of the 30th Annual ACM Symposium on Applied Computing* (ACM, 2015), pages 233–238
6. G.C. Challco, R. Mizoguchi, I.I. Bittencourt, S. Isotani, Gamification of collaborative learning scenarios: structuring persuasive strategies using game elements and ontologies, in *International Workshop on Social Computing in Digital Education* (Springer, 2015), pp. 12–28
7. R. Orji, R.L. Mandryk, J. Vassileva, Selecting effective strategies for tailoring persuasive health games to gamer types (2014)

8. R. Orji, R.L. Mandryk, J. Vassileva, K.M. Gerling, Tailoring persuasive health games to gamer type, in *Proceedings of the SIGCHI Conference on Human Factors in Computing Systems* (ACM, 2013), pp. 2467–2476
9. J. Masthoff, J. Vassileva, Tutorial on personalization for behaviour change, in *Proceedings of the 20th International Conference on Intelligent User Interfaces* (ACM, 2015), pp. 439–442
10. M. Meder, A. Rapp, T. Plumbaum, F. Hopfgartner, Data-driven gamification design, in *Proceedings of the 21st International Academic Mindtrek Conference* (ACM, 2017), pp. 255–258

Appendix
MeuTutor: Personalizing an Educational Technology Based on Students' Gamer Types

This appendix aims to present the appendices related to the Chap. 6 of this book.

A.1 Tailored Interfaces Based on Student's Gamer Types

(see Figs. A.1, A.2, A.3, A.4, A.5, A.6, A.7, A.8, A.9, A.10, A.11, A.12, A.13, A.14, A.15, A.16, A.17, A.18)

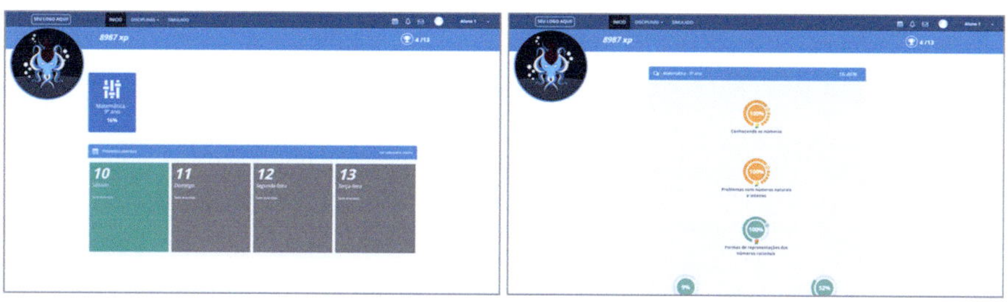

Fig. A.1 Tailored homepage and tree of activities for achiever students

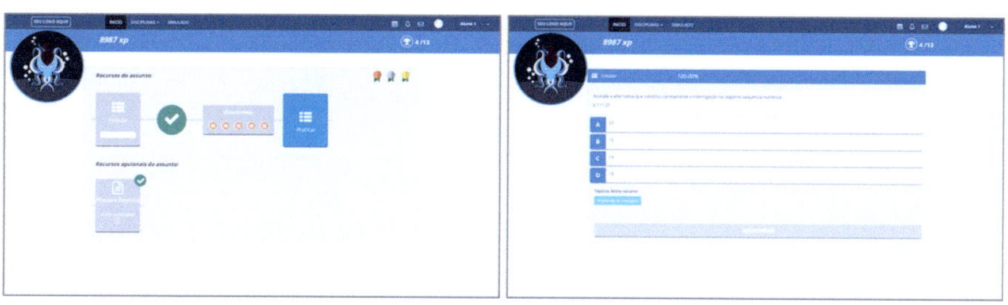

Fig. A.2 Tailored resources and specific activities for achiever students

W. Oliveira and I. I. Bittencourt, *Tailored Gamification to Educational Technologies*,
https://doi.org/10.1007/978-981-32-9812-5

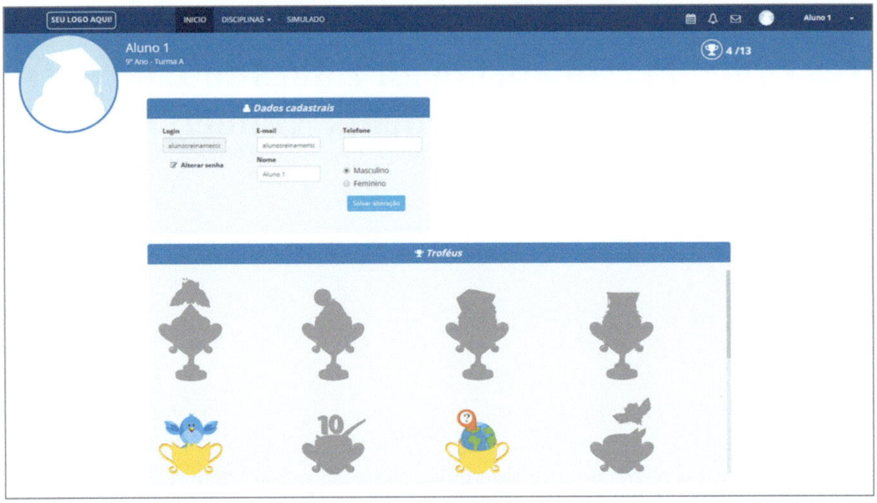

Fig. A.3 Tailored profile of the achiever gamer type

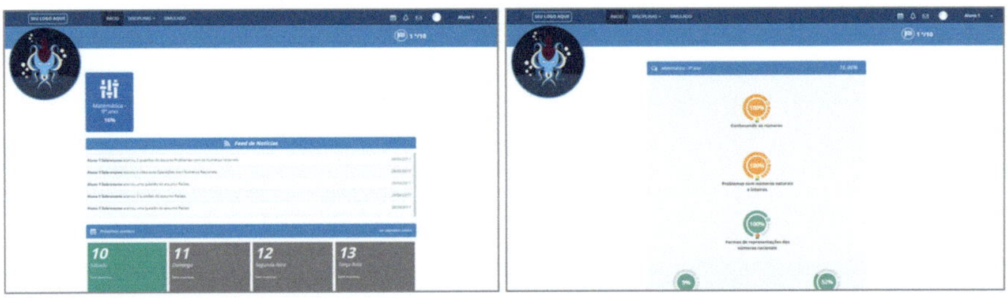

Fig. A.4 Tailored homepage and tree of activities for conqueror students

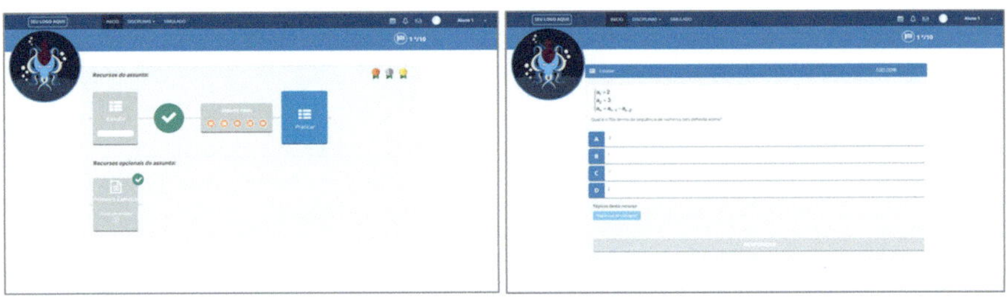

Fig. A.5 Tailored resources and specific activities for conqueror students

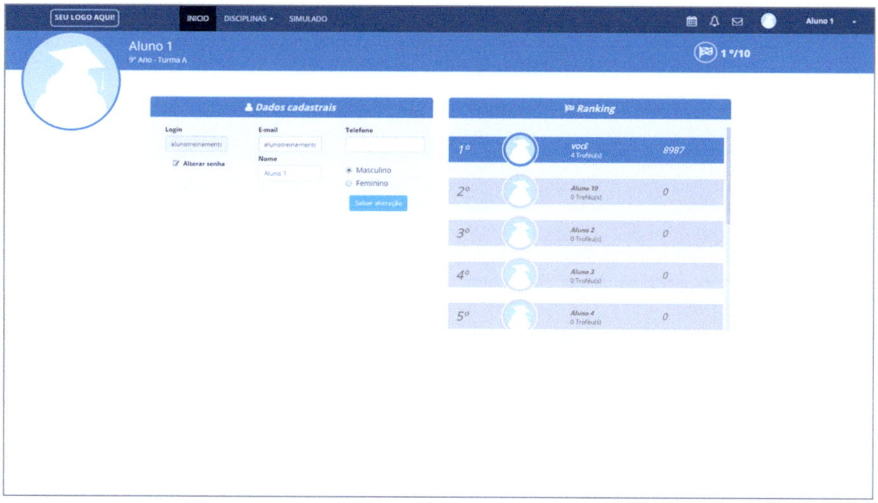

Fig. A.6 Tailored profile of the conqueror gamer type

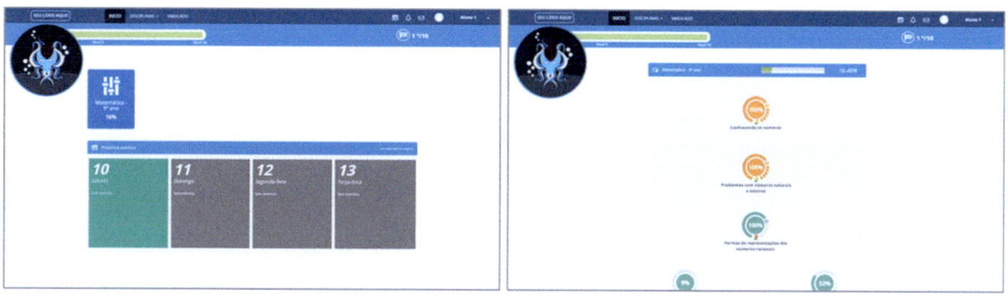

Fig. A.7 Tailored homepage and tree of activities for daredevil students

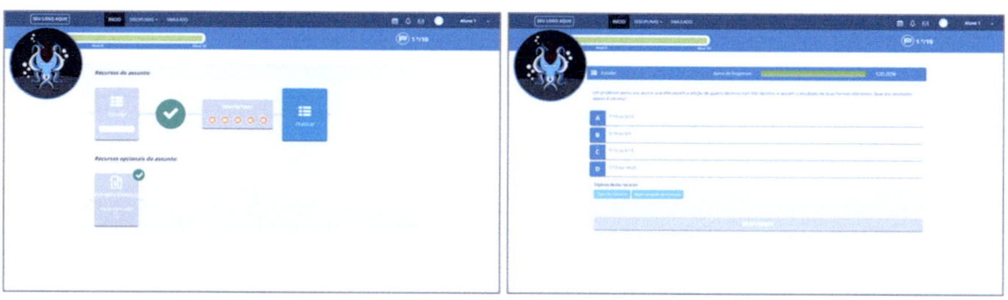

Fig. A.8 Tailored resources and specific activities for daredevil students

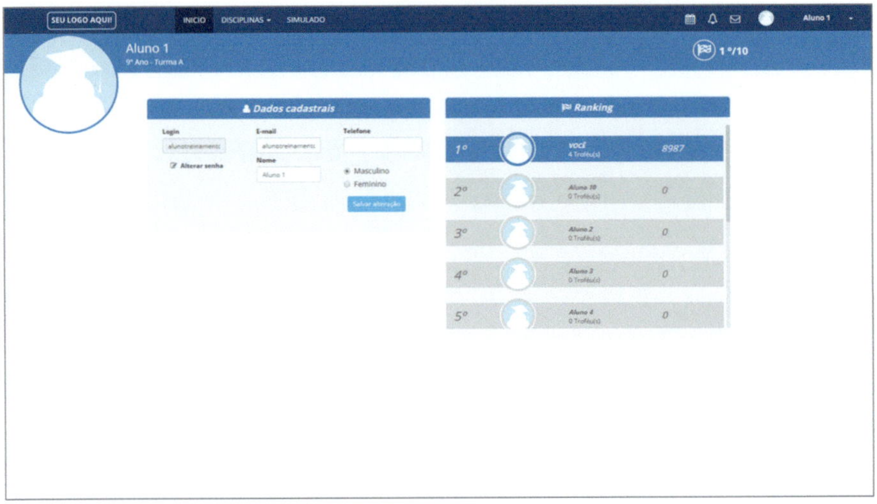

Fig. A.9 Tailored profile of the daredevil gamer type

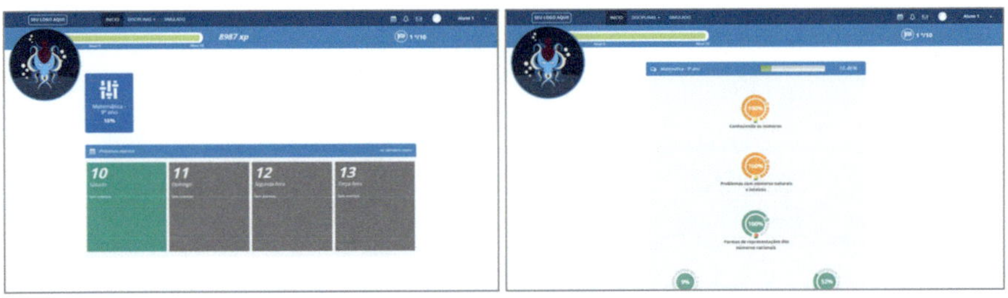

Fig. A.10 Tailored homepage and tree of activities for mastermind students

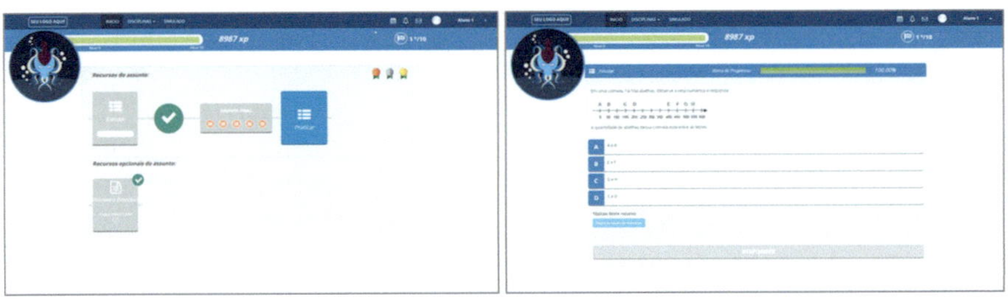

Fig. A.11 Tailored resources and specific activities for mastermind students

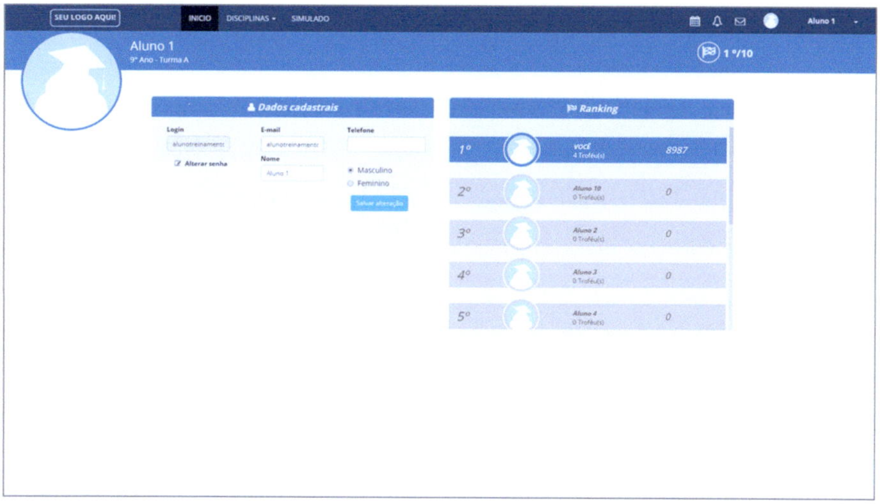

Fig. A.12 Tailored profile of the mastermind gamer type

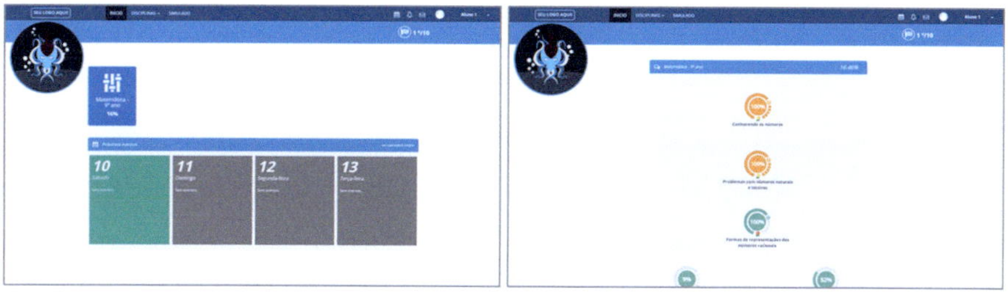

Fig. A.13 Tailored homepage and tree of activities for socializer students

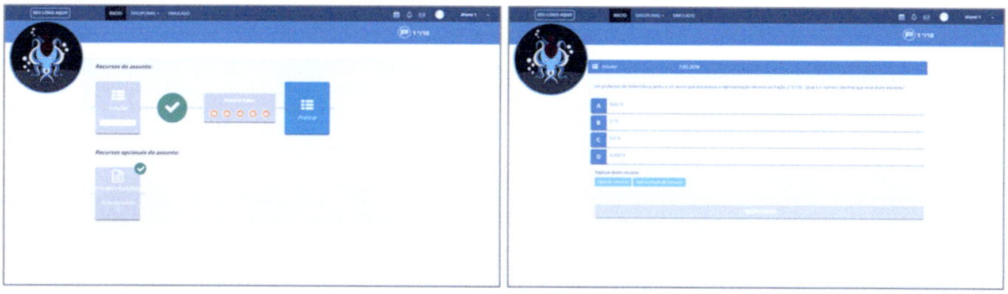

Fig. A.14 Tailored resources and specific activities for socializer students

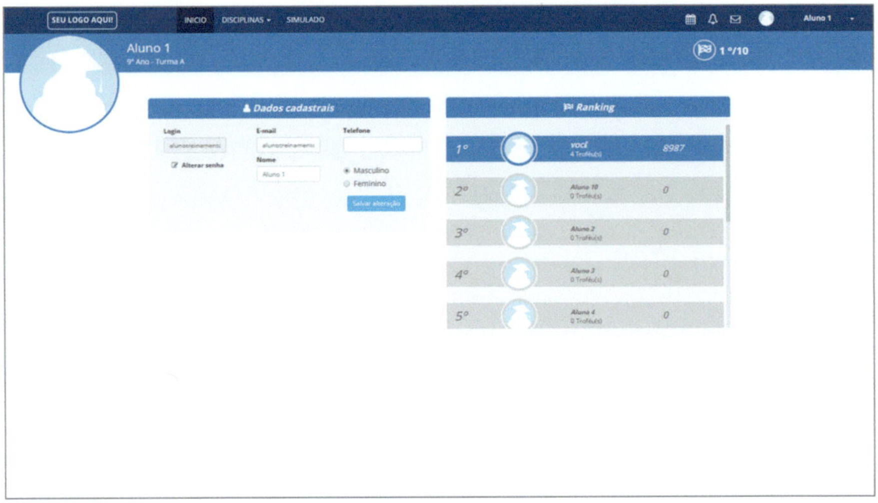

Fig. A.15 Tailored profile of the socializer gamer type

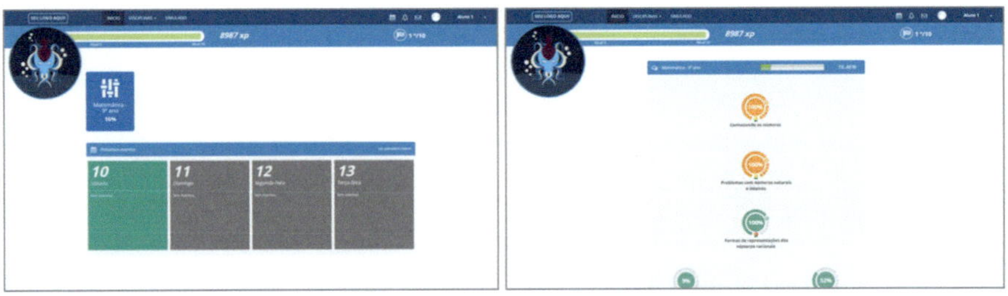

Fig. A.16 Tailored homepage and tree of activities for survivor students

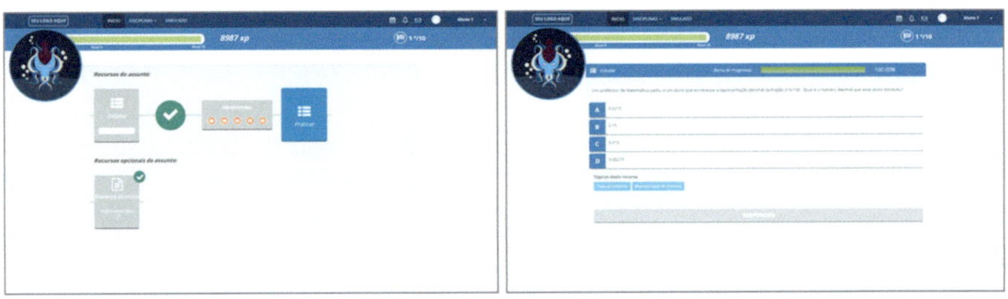

Fig. A.17 Tailored resources and specific activities for survivor students

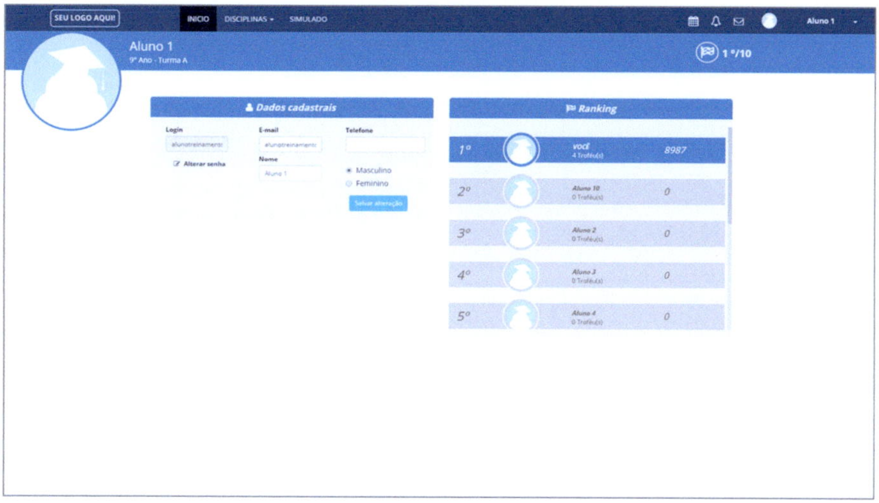

Fig. A.18 Tailored profile of the survivor gamer type

Glossary

Behaviorism Systematic approach to understanding the behavior of humans and other animals.

Cognitivism Theoretical framework for understanding the mind.

Constructivism Learning theory found in psychology which explains how people might acquire knowledge and learn.

Flow state Deep enjoyment experience.

Gameplay Specific way in which players interact with a game.

E-learning Learning conducted via electronic media, typically on the Internet.

Gamer type Classification of video game players.

One-size-fits-all Relating to policies or approaches that are standard and not tailored to individual needs.

Tailored gamification Gamification design personalized according to users characteristics.

W. Oliveira and I. I. Bittencourt, *Tailored Gamification to Educational Technologies*,
https://doi.org/10.1007/978-981-32-9812-5